A Shepherd Looks at

THE GOOD SHEPHERD

and His Sheep

D0972451

A Shepherd Looks at

THE GOOD SHEPHERD

and His Sheep

PHILLIP KELLER

**ZONDERVAN
PUBLISHING HOUSE** OF THE ZONDERVAN CORPORATION
GRAND RAPIDS, MICHIGAN 49506

To
Sidney Waterman
my friend, brother, and fellow adventurer
under God

A Shepherd Looks at the Good Shepherd and His Sheep
Copyright © 1978 by W. Phillip Keller

Sixth printing February 1981

Library of Congress Cataloging in Publication Data
Keller, Weldon Phillip, 1920-
   A shepherd looks at the Good Shepherd and His Sheep.
   Large print ed.
   1. Bible.   N.T.   John X—Meditations.   2. Large
type books.   I. Title.
[BS2615.4.K44   1979]   226'.5'077   79-4397
ISBN 0-310-26807-9

All rights reserved. No part of this publication may be reproduced, stored in a retrieval system, or transmitted in any form or by any means, electronic, mechanical, photocopy, recording or otherwise, without the prior permission of the copyright owner.

Illustrated by Nancy Munger

Printed in the United States of America

❖⟨ Contents ⟩❖

⚜ Acknowledgments ⚜

THIS IS TO express my genuine gratitude to my church for recording the messages upon which this work has been based. Those tapes, together with my own detailed study notes, comprise the background material for the book.

A note of appreciation is due also to my courageous wife, Ursula. She has taken great pains to type the manuscript carefully, correcting my wild spelling and making helpful suggestions. She, too, has encouraged me in my writing, when at times the pressure of so many responsibilities seemed almost too great to bear. I am grateful for her good cheer.

Lastly, I must thank Zondervan for their patience in waiting several years for this book to appear. May it be used in the hand of God to enrich and inspire those who read it quietly.

W. Phillip Keller

⊰ Preface ⊱

IT WAS AT the special request of the publishers that I undertook the writing of this book. It is intended as a companion piece to my previous work, *A Shepherd Looks at Psalm 23*.

That book has been used of God to enrich and inspire thousands of hearts and homes all over the world. It is my deep desire that the same may be true of this volume.

As with *A Shepherd Looks at Psalm 23*, this book also has first been shared in an extended series of lay lectures with my own congregation. In simple yet sincere studies the truths contained in John 10 have been passed on to seeking souls week after week. And out of those sessions our Lord has been pleased to bring enormous benefit to His people.

The fact that the Word of God first "comes alive" in the midst of people in public, reassures the writer that it can likewise "come alive" on the printed page for the reader in private. It was our great Shepherd Himself who stated emphatically, "The words that I speak unto you, they are spirit, and they are life" (John 6:63).

As with the book on Psalm 23, here, too, the Scriptures are explained from the standpoint of one who has been a sheep owner and sheep rancher. But beyond this they are examined by one who has enjoyed the care and companionship of the Good Shepherd, Christ our Lord, for many years.

It is the author's earnest prayer that these pages will open for the reader new vistas and wider horizons of understanding what God our Father, through Christ, by His gracious Spirit intends for His followers—the sheep of His care.

⋘ Setting the Stage ⋙

BEFORE WE BEGIN our study of this section of Scripture it is essential to set the stage in which our Lord stated the three parables contained in John 10. Only in this way can we comprehend clearly the truths He was teaching.

His own contemporaries, those to whom He addressed these ideas, were totally baffled by them. In fact, His hearers were so bewildered that some accused Him of being mad, or under the control of an evil spirit. They insisted that anyone making such statements as He made deserved death by stoning.

On the other hand there were those who, having just seen Him restore sight to the young man born blind, felt sure that what He said contained truth. It was bound to, since He could perform such miracles.

So it was that a storm of controversy raged around Christ. People were polarized by His parables. Some said He deserved to die. Others hailed Him as a Savior.

Down the long centuries of time since that desperate day in which He declared Himself to be the Good Shepherd, the controversy has continued over what He really meant. Scholars, teachers, theologians, academics, and preachers have all applied themselves to this passage of Scripture. Commentaries and books of various kinds have dealt with these parables. The diversity of views, and explanations given, leave one almost as perplexed as the people of Jesus' own time.

Consequently it is no easy thing to be invited to do a book on John 10. Yet it has been undertaken in humility and with the full knowledge of what others have written previously. It is not intended to discredit what has been drawn from these parables by other teachers. They are fully entitled to their views. But it should be said at the outset that the approach which I have taken is a very distinct, personal one. It is based, not on the concept of the nation Israel, referred to in the Old Testament as God's flock, the people of His fold; nor on the New Testament emphasis of the church being Christ's little flock; but rather on my simply belonging to Him as an individual.

The reasons for this are neither theological nor doctrinal. They are the practical realities of the setting and events in which these statements were made by Christ. And if, with open minds and gently receptive spirits we look at what transpired during the days immediately preceding this passage, it will be seen that the personal approach is valid.

Jesus was nearing the end of His public life. An increasing hostility was building up against Him from the ecclesiastical elite of His time. The religious leaders of His day felt threatened by His enormous popularity and appeal to the common people. The plain people applauded Him openly. His winsome words drew them with magnetic and positive power.

This continuous polarization around Christ created a constant storm center of controversy. The Scribes, Sadducees, and Pharisees tried every tactic to attack Him whenever He appeared in public. The masses on the other hand came to love Him with great affection.

His healing, helping, and heartening life had restored and lifted so many of them.

He entered Jerusalem to celebrate the Feast of Tabernacles, or Booths, with His men. It was a festival commemorating Jehovah's care of His people during their long wilderness wanderings after their exodus from Egypt. The Master immediately came under attack. In John 7 we see some claiming Him to be a "good man"; others insisting He was a "deceiver." And they would have lynched Him, if they could, but His hour of arrest had not yet come.

Then, on the last day of the feast He was assailed again. Some asserted He was truly "the Christ." His antagonists on the other hand claimed that Christ could not possibly come from Galilee. Officers were sent to arrest Him but failed to do so, declaring instead, "never man spake like this man!" So once more He was spared from the clutches of His opponents.

On the next day He returned to the city and was confronted by the Scribes and Pharisees with a young woman caught in an illicit sexual relationship. She was to be stoned, but to bait Jesus the frightened girl was brought to Him. Instead of condemning her, He forgave her but instructed her to go and sin no more.

The girl's accusers were furious. They engaged in a dreadful diatribe with Jesus in which He insisted upon His oneness with the Father. For this they again determined to stone Him to death. Yet He eluded them and escaped. All of this is described in John 8.

Later He was met by a man blind from birth. In a remarkable manner He touched the sightless eyes and the blind man saw when he went to bathe them in the pool of Siloam, as instructed. Out of deep gratitude the healed man gave glory and praise to his benefactor.

This precipitated another angry controversy with the religious skeptics and leaders.

Because he believed in the Christ the poor fellow was excommunicated from the religious life of his people. Jesus met him again and declared His own identity. The healed man was ecstatic and overwhelmed with adoration.

But to the Pharisees our Lord declared bluntly that they were both blind and steeped in sin and self-righteousness. All their religiosity had done them not one bit of good.

It is on this pathetic theme that John 9 concludes.

In blazing, bold contrast, Christ had personally touched and entered both the lives of the young adulteress and this supposedly sinful, blind man. He had brought them into an intimate, new relationship of abundant living with Himself.

Put into the language of the New Testament, these two individuals had discovered what is meant by "Christ in me," and "I in Christ." They had both entered into that dynamic new dimension of living which Christ Himself later referred to as "[Abiding] in me, and I in you."

To depict and dramatize this remarkable relationship with Himself He then proceeded to tell the three parables of the Shepherd and His sheep in the next chapter.

By contrast, in Psalm 23, David the author writes from the standpoint of a sheep speaking about its owner. In John 10 the approach is the opposite. Our Lord, Jesus the Christ, here speaks as the Good Shepherd. He describes His relationship to His sheep; we, the common people, who have come into His ownership and under His care.

PARABLE I

John 10:1-5

CHRIST IN ME

❧ 1 ❧
The
Sheepfold

Verily, verily I say unto you, He that entereth not by the door into the sheepfold, but climbeth up some other way, the same is a thief and a robber. (John 10:1)

WHAT IS A sheepfold?

It is an enclosure open to the wind.

It is an enclosure open to the scrutiny of the owner.

It is an enclosure *not* covered in, roofed over, or shielded from the eyes of the shepherd.

It is not a barn, shed, or closed-in structure.

Its walls, open to the sun, the sky, stars, rain, and wind may be made of rough-laid stones, sun-dried bricks,

timber, mud and wattle, or even tightly packed thorn brush, called a corral in some places, a kraal in others, and a boma in parts of Africa.

The main purpose of the sheepfold is to provide protection for the sheep—especially at night and in stormy weather. Its high thick walls are a barrier that prevents thieves or, to use a modern parlance, rustlers from invading the flock to plunder the defenseless sheep.

The enclosing walls are also a safeguard for the sheep against all sorts of predators. These vary, depending upon the country in which the sheep are kept. In some areas it is a case of keeping out wolves or jackals. In others, especially parts of Africa, lions, leopards, and even hyenas are guarded against.

Even then, despite the barricade of thorn brush, there are occasions when predators will prowl around a sheepfold stealthily searching for some spot where they can leap over the enclosure to capture and kill their prey. This produces panic among the flock. The carnage is terrifying and the losses among the flock can be enormous. For the sheep owner the raids on his sheep represent serious financial reverses which may take years to recover.

I had a neighbor whose flock was raided one night by a cougar. By daybreak more than thirty of his finest ewes lay dead on the ground. Fences and walls had been cleared by the powerful predator without it ever passing through a gate or open door.

"Sheepfold," besides being the name for an enclosure where sheep are generally kept at night, is also a term for managing sheep. In sheep countries we often speak freely of "folding" sheep. By that we mean the much wider sense in which a flock of sheep are said to be "enfolded" by a certain owner or sheepman. The sheep come under his special management and his direct control continuously. He folds his flock exactly as he sees fit in order that they will flourish and prosper under his care.

Folding sheep is another way of saying a shepherd is managing his flock with maximum skill. It is to say that he handles them with expertise, moving them from field to field, pasture to pasture, range to range in order to benefit them as much as he can, as well as to enhance his own land.

So a sheepfold conveys the idea of the special relationship a sheep has to the ownership and care of a certain shepherd. And when our Lord, who referred to Himself as the Good Shepherd spoke these parables, He saw the overall picture of the unique relationship between Himself and His followers—between Himself and those who had come under His good hand for the management of their lives.

He begins this first parable by asserting that anyone who forces a way into the "sheepfold" other than by the proper doorway or entrance may be a thief or robber. In other words, He is saying that my life is a sheepfold to which He alone, the Good Shepherd, is the rightful owner.

Within the fold of my life there are all kinds of people who come in and out. There are the members of my immediate family circle, my wife, children, grandchildren, cousins, or more distant relatives. Then there are friends, neighbors, business associates, schoolmates or strangers who from time to time pass in and out of the circle of my life.

In reality none of our lives are totally closed in, roofed over, and so completely sealed and safeguarded as to forestall the entry of others. Each of us is a sheepfold in his own private, individual way. We are within a fold, a circle, a life, which really cannot be roofed over.

It is true some of us may have high walls of self-defense erected around us. We may even go so far as to try and enclose ourselves completely to forestall invasion from others, and we may feel we have actually succeeded in this. However, we may fool ourselves into believing that we can withdraw into our own secluded little domain where we are exempt from the entrance and intrusion of others.

Christ's assertion is that in fact this is simply not possible. It is true I am in an enclosure. It is true I live within a limited circle which, however, is shared by others who enter it. But over and beyond this my life is surrounded and enfolded by the encircling care and provision of a providential God. Nor is it closed off from His loving care and concern. It is in fact wide open to the wind—the wind of His gracious Spirit. There is no way He can be kept out, any more than the wind blowing across the countryside can be kept out of an open sheepfold.

The truth that there is no one anywhere who can escape or elude the coming of God's Spirit, is portrayed in exquisite detail in Psalm 139. There is no way known to man in which he can prevent the gracious presence of God's Spirit from making an impact on the fold of his life. We are surrounded by Him; we are found by Him; we are touched by Him. His impact is upon us. We are beneath the influence of His hand . . . His person . . . His presence!

O LORD, thou hast searched me, and known me.
Thou knowest my downsitting and mine uprising,
  thou understandest my thought afar off.
Thou compassest my path and my lying down,
  and art acquainted with all my ways.
For there is not a word in my tongue, but,
  lo, O LORD, thou knowest it altogether.
Thou hast beset me behind and before,
  and laid thine hand upon me.
Such knowledge is too wonderful for me;
  it is high, I cannot attain unto it.
Whither shall I go from thy spirit?
  or whither shall I flee from thy presence?
If I ascend up into heaven, thou art there:
  if I make my bed in hell, behold, thou art there.
If I take the wings of the morning, and dwell
  in the uttermost parts of the sea;
Even there shall thy hand lead me,
  and thy right hand shall hold me.
If I say, Surely the darkness shall cover me;
  even the night shall be light about me.
Yea, the darkness hideth not from thee;
  but the night shineth as the day:
The darkness and the light are both alike to thee.
                              (Ps. 139:1-12)

In the light of all this we must conclude quietly that
though we may be able to exclude others from our
lives, to a degree, we cannot do this with Christ. He
comes to us again and again seeking entry.

He does not force His way in. He does not gate-crash
my life or yours. He chooses to enter by the proper
entrance which is really His privilege. Yet He is so
gracious in requesting our cooperation in this.

Still, in fear and apprehension we often exclude
Him, while at the same time, unknowingly, we are
invaded by adversaries.

Many who force their way into my life, who slip in
by means that are cunning, who impose themselves by

25

devious and destructive tactics, often are bent on deceiving and destroying me. They are thieves and predators who are determined to plunder and exploit me as a person for their own selfish ends.

We live in a world and society rife with those who hold and propagate false teachings, false philosophies, false idealogies, false concepts, false values, and false standards of behavior. We are approached on every side by those who would penetrate our lives to pillage them if they could. Their aim is to exploit us. They would rob us of the rich benefits which could be ours as the sheep of God's pasture.

Sad to say that in many lives they have actually succeeded. People have been pillaged. Countless lives have been robbed by the enemy posing as proper owners. Yet in those same lives, in those very sheepfolds, the door has never been opened to the Good Shepherd who really does have the right to enter, and who in truth is entitled to their ownership and care.

This is one of the enduring enigmas of human behavior that is so baffling. We human beings will allow all kinds of strange ideologies and philosophies to permeate our thinking. We will allow humanistic standards and materialistic concepts to actually rob us of the finest values that would otherwise enrich us. We permit false aims and ambitions to penetrate our thinking and dominate our desires, scarcely aware that in so doing we are forfeiting the richest values our Good Shepherd intended for us.

On every side we see people robbed, not necessarily of materialistic possessions, but of the much more enduring assets of eternal worth and duration.

The simple solution to this whole dilemma is to discover for ourselves that in truth the only One who

26

really has a right to manage the fold of my life is not myself, but God.

Most of us labor under the delusion that we have every right to our lives; that we have the right to go where we wish, do as we please, live as we choose, and decide our own destiny. We do not. We belong to God. He made us for Himself. He chose us in Christ out of love, from before the foundation of the earth to be His own. He has bought us twice over, both through His generous death and also by His amazing resurrection life.

Every faculty I possess in my body, mind, emotions, will, disposition, and spirit has been entrusted to me as a gift, bestowed by the bounty of a generous, gracious, self-giving, self-sharing God in Christ. There is no such thing as a "self-made" man or woman. To assert this is colossal conceit of the first magnitude. It is an affront to the living Lord who alone has a rightful claim on me.

Even the total earth environment, the biota, of which I am a part, and which sustains me during my brief earth sojourn is God's doing. Only at His pleasure is it maintained in perfect balance and poise. It provides the precise support mechanisms which insure my survival upon this sphere in space.

Now Christ is the visible expression of the invisible God. He was born before creation began, for it was through him that everything was made, whether heavenly or earthly, seen or unseen. Through him, and for him, also, were created power and dominion, ownership and authority. In fact, all things were created through, and for, him. He is both the first principle and the upholding principle of the whole scheme of creation. (Col. 1:15-17, Phillips)

In view of the fact that all of life originates with Christ we should be able to see the reasonableness of admitting His ownership of us. We ought to discern the inescapable conclusion that He is entitled to enfold us with His loving care and concern. We should recognize the fact that He is fully and uniquely qualified to manage us with a skill and understanding far surpassing our own.

In spite of all this He does not insist on imposing Himself upon us. He does not override our wills. He refuses to rush into our experience by gate-crashing His way over our decisions. Having made us in His own likeness, free-will agents able to choose as we wish, whether or not we shall be His sheep, enfolded in His care, is ultimately up to us. This is a staggering decision facing each individual.

The amazing generosity of Christ in so approaching us stills our spirits and awes our souls before Him. Yet at the same time He insists anyone else who attempts to invade my life as an imposter, a counterfeit shepherd, is in truth none other than a thief and a robber . . . a plunderer of my life who will impoverish and cripple me.

2

The Shepherd's Entry

But he that entereth in by the door is the shepherd of the sheep. To him the porter openeth. (John 10:2-3a)

BECAUSE THE SHEEPFOLD belongs to the shepherd who constructed it, he has the right to use and enter it as he wishes. The sheep who occupy it belong to him. The sheepfold is an integral part of his complete sheep operation. The flock moves in and out through the entrance either to find security by night or fresh fields for grazing by day.

Whenever the shepherd comes to the fold it is for the benefit of the sheep. Unlike the rustlers or predators who come to raid or rob the livestock within, he always comes with beneficial intentions. The sheep do not fear him. They do not flee in panic or rush about in bewildered confusion, trampling and maiming each other in blind excitement.

In fact, some of my most winsome recollections of handling livestock during my long life are wrapped around those poignant moments of watching an owner come to his stock. Some come with gentle calls. They alert the sheep that they are approaching. Others whistle gaily as they near the gate so as to set the sheep at ease. Some sheepmen and sheepherders in Africa love to sing soft plaintive tunes as they come to the corral or sheepfold.

All of these approaches are diametrically opposite of the sly, subtle tactics of the predators or prowlers who attempt to pounce on their prey by surprise. They want to catch the sheep off-guard and capture them amid their confusion. It is a crafty, cunning part of their plan of attack.

And when the shepherd reaches the entrance it is customary to tap on the gate, or rattle the latch, or knock on the door loud enough so that all within the enclosure are alerted to the fact that he is outside, ready to enter. More than this, he expects to enter.

When we apply this concept to our own lives we see the striking parallels. So often in our past we have seen our lives exploited by those who had only their own selfish interests at heart. They were not in the least concerned what happened to us as long as their own insidious, greedy ends were gained. They used and abused their prey to promote their own designs, no matter how much destruction they wrought.

By contrast there is none of this in Christ, the great Good Shepherd. Because of His care and concern for us, because of His self-giving love and conduct He comes to us always with peaceable intentions. All through the long and painful history of the human race we see God coming to willful, wayward men in peace.

Always His words of introduction to us are: "Peace be with you"; "Peace be unto you!"; "Be not afraid, it is I"; "Peace, good will toward men!"; "Peace I leave with you . . . not as the world giveth, give I unto you!"

He does not come to men to plunder or prey upon them. God has never exploited any person. Not once has He extracted anything from anyone for His own ends. There is not even a hint of grasping greed regarding the Good Shepherd who approaches us only with our best interests in mind. He does not use people for some selfish pleasure of His own.

And because He comes to us in generous good will He comes gently and graciously. He is Jesus the Christ; "The perfect Gentleman!" He refuses to force His way into our lives. In His magnanimity He created us in His own image with free wills, able to act independently in determining our own decisions.

He stands outside our lives, entreating us gently to grant Him admission. The generosity of such an approach overwhelms us when we pause to reflect that in truth He really has every right to enter.

The enormous pathos of this appeal by Christ to our human hearts is portrayed vividly by the aged and beloved John writing in the third chapter of Revelation. There God's Spirit speaks to us,

See, I am now standing at the door and knocking. If any one listens to My voice and opens the door, I will come in to him and feast (share life) with him, and he shall feast with Me.   (Rev. 3:20, *Weymouth*)

This One who so entreats us to open our lives to His

31

entrance is none other than God very God, the Christ, who in the second parable of John 10 declares emphatically "I am the good shepherd. . . . I am come that they might have life, and that they might have it more abundantly!"

He comes to us anticipating an entrance. He is entitled to enter and has that privilege because He is our rightful owner. This will be explained later in this chapter.

There is a gross misunderstanding among many as to what God's intentions may be in expecting entry into our lives. They assume He will make enormous demands upon them which cannot be fulfilled. They imagine they will be deprived of pleasures or practices which will leave them poorer people. Beleaguered by such misconceptions they are reluctant to grant Him admission.

Yet, the opposite is true of the Good Shepherd. He seeks entry to enrich us. He desires to put at our disposal all of His wondrous resources. He wants to inject an exciting new dimension of dynamic living into our days. He intends to share His very life with us. Out of that life imparted to me as an individual can come all the noble qualities of a fine and wholesome life which are uniquely His. These are made real in me, by His presence. They are further transmitted through me to touch other lives bringing blessing and benefit to those around me.

Why then are we still so loathe to let Him in?

There are various reasons, of which two far transcend all the others.

The first of these is fear. Almost all of us have at some time or other allowed people into our lives who took unfair advantage of us. They have hurt and wounded us. Sometimes they have abused us callously and with great cruelty. We started out trusting them to a degree, and ended up torn and mutilated by the encounter.

The end result is that we begin to build high walls of self-defense and self-preservation around ourselves. We want to protect ourselves from the onslaught of outsiders. If perchance we have been injured repeatedly we become even more wary, cautious, and unwilling to open ourselves to anyone whom we regard as an intruder.

We bluntly warn people, "I don't want you in my life!"; "Please stay away, I don't want you interfering in my affairs"; "Just keep out of my business and mind your own"; "Live your life and let me live mine."

And though we may not say so in actual words, we entertain the same attitude toward Christ when He comes to call at the doorway of our hearts (i.e., our wills). We subconsciously attribute to Him the same selfish motives and ulterior designs which characterize selfish human beings.

This is, of course, unfair to God. But it also demonstrates that we really do not know or understand Him, for His thoughts toward us are always good.

> For I know the thoughts that I think toward you, saith the LORD, thoughts of peace, and not of evil, to give you an expected end. (Jer. 29:11)

And the ultimate end He has in mind for me is that my will should be aligned with His; my life moving in harmony with His; together sharing in the magnificent plans and purposes He has for His people. To so live is to enter a powerful, positive adventure of selfless giving of ourselves for the good of all. This is the great dynamic of the love of God at work throughout the whole cosmos. It is the divine energy that drives the universe!

Yet most of us will not respond to His overtures. We prefer to draw back, to close ourselves off from Christ, to withdraw within the closely confining circle of our selfish little lives. There we feel more secure and self-assured. It is comfortable and we prefer this confinement—even if we are cramped within the con-stricting walls of our own making and choice.

The second reason why people will not open up their lives to the Good Shepherd is much more subtle and insidious. It is an integral part of our lifelong condi-tioning and culture to assume that I, Me, My, are enti-tled to absolute priority in our thinking, planning, and conduct.

From earliest childhood we insist on having our own way, indulging our own desires, doing our own thing, going our own way with our wishes always para-mount. We become veritable little "kings in our own castles," or even worse, "little gods in the temples of our own lives." We resent anyone who dares to enter our domain. We even naively assume at times we can be "the shepherd in our own fold."

There is no doubt in our minds that we are entitled to make all our own decisions, no matter how disas-trous the consequences. We are sure we can solve all our dilemmas even though they lead us deeper and deeper into despair. We are determined to run our own lives even if we run them into the ground, ending up in absolute ruin.

In all of this we are positive no one else can manage our affairs nor control our conduct any better than we can. In pride and self-will we view outsiders, God included, as intruders, imposters who dare to try and usurp control. And we adamantly refuse them entrance.

As I sometimes say to people who take up this fortified position, "You have not only erected high walls around your life; you have dug a deep moat outside and drawn up the drawbridge lest anyone ever come in."

In spite of our indifference, our fear, our pride, our determined refusal to let Him in, Christ is very patient and compassionate with us. He keeps coming. He keeps speaking. He keeps standing at the door. He keeps knocking. He keeps rattling the latch.

In the case of a few lives the door is finally opened. Our Lord made the unusual comment that it was really the "porter," the doorkeeper who opens the door. And it may well be asked, "Who is the porter? Who is this One who for the sake and welfare of the sheep opens up the sheepfold to the Good Shepherd?"

He is none other than the gracious Spirit of God Himself. It is He who, unbeknown to us, and long before we are conscious of the presence of Christ, comes to us quietly to begin His gentle work within. It is He who gradually prevails upon our spirits to respond. It is He who, even in our willful waywardness, is at work within us turning us toward the One who stands outside the fold of our lives. It is He who gradually overcomes our fears, our deep subconscious inhibitions toward Christ. He is able in His own wondrous way to pulverize our pride, to lead us gently to see the enormous folly of our self-centeredness. He generates within our wills the active faith needed to comply with and respond to the voice of the Good Shepherd.

It is then and only then that the door is opened to

Christ. It is then that the guard, so to speak, is let down. Then the One outside is granted entry. For some this is an act of great apprehension. It involves a definite movement within the will. Yet it is God who works within us to will and to do of His good pleasure. (See Phil. 2:13.)

In his autobiography C. S. Lewis tells how he had long resisted the gentle overtures of Christ to enter his life. One day, while riding atop a double-decker bus to the zoo in London, he sensed he could no longer keep the Lord out of his life. By a definite, deliberate act of his will he literally unfastened the defenses within which he had enclosed himself for so long. Then the presence and the person of Christ moved quietly, but wondrously, into his soul. He was instantly "surprised by joy." And this phrase is the title of his book.

When Christ enters He brings not only joy, peace, and reassurance to the opened heart; He brings also the divine resources of love, life, light, and fullness of character which are uniquely His. These are essential to the new life style He initiates. It is He who assumes control. It is He who begins to manage the sheep. It is He who begins to give direction and purpose to all that happens to them.

Of course it can be asked, "Is He really entitled to do this?" "Is He my rightful owner?" "Does He have the credentials to determine what shall be done with my life?" To each of these the emphatic reply is yes!

First of all, we must be reminded that it is He who made us. The amazing intricacy of our bodies; the incredible potential of our minds and memories; the enormous capacities of our emotions; the unmeasurable impact of our wills; the unplumbed depths of our spirits . . . each and all are glorious gifts bestowed upon us in generosity by God. We did not fashion or form them. They belong rightfully to Him. They are simply entrusted to us for wise use under His direction for the brief duration of our days on earth.

Secondly, though all of us in willful, self-centered waywardness have gone our way to do as we want, we are invited to return to Him and to come under His care. To make this possible, He has brought us back with His own life, given in sacrifice for us. So in reality He has redeemed us, brought us back, made it possible to be accepted again as His own.

Thirdly, He continues ever to intercede on our behalf. He suffers in our stead. He entreats us to become wholly His in glad abandon.

So it is that on this basis it is both reasonable and proper that, as His own people, the sheep of His pasture, we have every obligation to throw open wide the door of our lives, allowing Him to enter gladly as our Lord, our Shepherd.

3

The
Shepherd's Voice

And the sheep hear his voice: and he calleth his own
sheep by name, and leadeth them out. (John 10:3b)

THE RELATIONSHIP WHICH rapidly develops between a
shepherd and the sheep under his care is to a definite
degree dependent upon the use of the shepherd's
voice. Sheep quickly become
accustomed to their own-
er's particular voice.
They are acquainted
with its unique tone.
They know its pecu-
liar sounds and
inflections.

They can distinguish it from that of any other person.

If a stranger should come among them, they would not recognize nor respond to his voice in the same way they would to that of the shepherd. Even if the visitor should use the same words and phrases as that of their rightful owner they would not react in the same way. It is a case of becoming actually conditioned to the familiar nuances and personal accent of their shepherd's call.

It used to amaze and intrigue visitors to my ranches to discover that my sheep were so indifferent to their voices. Occasionally I would invite them to call my sheep using the same words and phrases which I habitually employed. But it was to no avail. The ewes and lambs, and even the rams, would simply stand and stare at the newcomers in rather blank bewilderment, as if to say, "Who are you?"

This is simply because over a period of time sheep come to associate the sound of the shepherd's voice with special benefits. When the shepherd calls to them it is for a specific purpose that has their own best interests in mind. It is not something he does just to indulge himself or to pass the time away.

His voice is used to announce his presence; he is there. It is to allay their fears and timidity. Or it is to call them to himself so they can be examined and counted carefully. He wants to make sure that they are all well, fit, and flourishing. Sometimes the voice is used to announce that fresh feed is being supplied, or salt, minerals, or water. He might call them up to lead them into fresh pastures or into some shelter from an approaching storm. But always the master's call conveys to the sheep a positive assurance that he cares for them and is acting in their best interests.

When my children were young they saved up their few dollars to purchase their own pet ewes. And it was a delight to watch them go out to the fields and call up their own sheep. Quickly these ewes came to recognize the voice of their owners. When they were called they would come running to be given some special little hand-out of grain or green grass. They would be hugged and cuddled and caressed with childish delight. It was something which both the sheep and the owners enjoyed.

In all of this the key to the contentment of the sheep lies in recognizing the owner's voice. When the sheep hear that voice they know it is their master and respond at once. And the response is much more than one of mere recognition. They actually run toward the shepherd. They come to him for they know he has something good for them.

In examining the Christian life we discover powerful parallels. We find that at some time or other most of us have heard God's voice. We knew the Good Shepherd was calling. As our Lord Himself said so often when He was here among men, "If any man hear my voice," then certain things would happen.

But first the question may well be asked, "How does one hear God's voice?" "Is it possible for Him to communicate with me?" The simple answer is Yes; definitely.

He may speak to me clearly through His Word, whereby He has chosen to articulate Himself. His own gracious Spirit will impress upon my spirit His intentions and purposes for me as a person.

He may do this privately in the quiet seclusion of my own home, in the stillness of my devotions. He may, on the other hand, do it through some message spoken from a church pulpit, through a radio broadcast or a television program.

Christ may come and speak to me through a devout and godly friend, neighbor, or family member. He may call to me clearly through some magazine, periodical, or book I have read. An ever-deepening conviction and awareness that this or that is what I "ought to do," may come to me. This great "I ought to" or "I ought not" is the growing compulsion of His inner voice speaking to me in unmistakable accents by His Spirit.

The Lord has chosen to articulate Himself also through the splendor and beauty of His created universe. The psalmist portrays this for us in exquisite poetry.

> The heavens declare the glory (character) of God; and the firmament sheweth his handiwork. Day unto day uttereth speech, and night unto night sheweth knowledge. There is no speech nor language, where their *voice* is not heard. Their line is gone out through all the earth, and their words to the end of the world.
>
> (Ps. 19:1-4)

He also communicates with me clearly through the wondrous character, conduct, and conversation of Christ Himself. He, "the Word," became flesh and dwelled among us. Through His flawless life, His impeccable character, His wondrous words I can hear God's voice. He asserted boldly and without apology, "The words that I speak unto you, they are spirit, and they are life" (John 6:63). On another occasion He insisted, "I am the way, the truth, and the life: no man cometh unto the Father, but by me" (John 14:6).

From the foregoing it is obvious that anyone can hear God's voice; it is possible for us to be reached. But the burning question of communication is, Do we hear? By that I mean much more than merely making contact. This was a perpetual point of pain to our Master when He was among men. Over and over His comment was, "Ears you have, but you hear not!"

Hearing is much more involved, much more complex than it appears on the surface. It embraces more than just being spoken to by God. It involves three very definite aspects of interaction with Him.

If, in actual fact Christ the Good Shepherd has been granted entry into the little fold of my life, then I will have begun to become familiar with His voice. This then implies that I do *recognize* His voice. I learn to distinguish it from the many other voices calling to me amid a confused society and a complex world. I come to that awareness where I am alert and attuned to the special attributes of Christ's call to me personally. I am like young Samuel who, in response to the voice of God, replied, "Speak, Lord, for thy servant heareth."

O great Shepherd, I am listening. I am attentive. I am waiting for Your word to me. I am ready to recognize what You have to say to me.

The second aspect to hearing God's voice is that I *respond* to it. He chooses to communicate with me in order to impress upon me His intentions and desires. He has good intentions toward me. They are in my own best interests and it is incumbent upon me that I recognize this, take them seriously, and respond accordingly.

The instant sheep hear and recognize their shepherd's voice, they lift their heads, turn in the direction from which the sound comes, and cock their ears to catch every syllable. Whether resting, feeding, or fighting, everything else is forgotten for the moment

43

because they have heard their owner's call. It commands their full and undivided attention. Something new and different is about to happen.

The same should be true of us in responding to God's voice. It should command our undivided attention. We should never allow the other interests and demands of our often busy lives to blur the gentle appeals that come to us from Christ. He does not blow mighty bugles to gain our attention. We are not hounds being called to the hunt, but sheep being lead in the paths of righteousness. If we are not sensitive to the overtures of His Spirit and quickly responsive to the distinct promptings of His Word, we are not going to go anywhere with Him.

It is often frustrating to a shepherd when he calls his sheep to discover that though they may have recognized his voice and responded to it, they still refuse to move. They simply will not come running when called.

Again and again I have watched a flock of sheep in which there were a few recalcitrant ones. Standing there stupidly and stubbornly they simply shake their heads, waggle their ears, and bleat out a pathetic "blah!" For the shepherd calling them, this is frustrating.

The same thing is too often true among God's people. We recognize His voice, we respond to it to a degree, but we will not move. We will not act. We will not run to Him. We adamantly refuse to comply with His wishes or cooperate with His intentions for us.

Our attitude and actions are as absurd as any "Blah!" bleated by some stupid, stubborn sheep. We stand still, not moving a step toward Him who is so fond of us. We appear to be almost paralyzed . . . impotent to move a step ahead in the will of God.

Now the reader may well ask, "How does a person move toward Christ? How does he, so to speak, 'run to do His will'?" It is obvious that if we are to benefit from hearing His voice we must step out to do what He calls us to do.

This involves much more than merely giving mental assent to what we may have heard. It simply is not enough just to agree with what God's Spirit may have said to us. It goes far beyond even becoming emotionally exercised about what we have heard. It is possible for people to weep tears of bitterness or remorse yet never move toward God. It is equally ineffective for individuals to become merely ecstatic about some spiritual issue, for, when the emotion has passed, they are still standing precisely where they were before the call came from Christ.

What then is the step needed to move us? It is an action of our will. It is the deliberate *choice* of our disposition to *do that which we have been called to do.*

We refer to this as the *response of faith in action.* It is the compliance of our will to God's will through straightforward obedience and glad cooperation.

Truth becomes truth to me, and spiritual life becomes spiritual life to me only when I actually do the thing Christ calls me to do!

Not until this actually takes place do we move toward the Shepherd or begin to experience the benefits of His care and management. We may know all about Him in a theoretical, doctrinal way. But actually living, walking, and communing with Him in a personal encounter will be something foreign and unknown.

Unfortunately many who call themselves Christians, who consider themselves the followers of Christ, who claim to be the sheep of His flock, are really still strangers to His voice. They have yet to know the precious and special delight of actually *knowing Him.*

Our Lord referred to this in a solemn statement He made in the Sermon on the Mount. It is full of pathos and poignant pain: "Not every one that saith unto me, Lord, Lord, shall enter into the kingdom of heaven; but *he that doeth the will of my Father which is in heaven.* Many will say unto me in that day Lord, Lord. . . . And then will I profess unto them I *never knew you"* (Matt. 7:21-23).

The relationship between the shepherd and his sheep, between Christ and those whom He calls, is one of personal, profound *knowing;* for He knows me intimately, He knows me by name.

Only those who are acquainted with the pastoral life of a sheep owner in the Middle East or Africa are able to grasp how thoroughly these people know their livestock. Their livestock are their very life. Sheep, goats, cattle, camels, and donkeys are both the center and circumference of their entire social scene.

If one goes to visit a village, the order of greeting and salutation is first to ask how the owner himself is faring. Then one inquires after the health of his sheep and cattle. Following that one asks about his children, then lastly his wife or wives. This is not intended as any slur on his family, but it does point up the enormous importance attached to livestock. They are the paramount consideration in the life of the owner.

A second remarkable aspect of the care of animals in these countries is that each one is known by name. These names are not simple common names such as we might choose. Rather, they are complex and unique because they have some bearing upon the history of the individual beast. For example, an ewe might be

46

called: "The one born in the dry river bed," or "The beautiful lamb for which I traded two pots of honey."

During the years when my family and I lived among the Masai people of East Africa I was deeply moved by the intense devotion and affection shown by the owners for their stock. Out in the grazing lands or beside the watering places they would call their pets by name, and it was sheer joy to watch their response as they came to the shepherd's call to be examined, handled, fondled, petted, and adored.

Some of these sheep had literally grown up as members of the family household. From their earliest days they had been cuddled, hugged, fed, and loved like one of the owner's own children. Every minute detail of their lives was well known and fully understood.

A remarkable picture of this is portrayed for us in 2 Samuel 12:3, where the prophet of God rebuked King David for his adultery with Bathsheba, when he likened Uriah to a poor shepherd with only one little lamb.

> But the poor man had nothing, save one little ewe lamb, which he had bought and nourished up: and it grew up together with him, and with his children; it did eat of his own meat, and drank of his own cup, and lay in his bosom, and was unto him as a daughter.

Is it any wonder that such ewes and lambs were called by endearing names? It is little marvel that every detail of their lives, every unusual facet of their character was known intimately.

This is the picture portrayed for us by Christ when He made the terse statement: "He calleth his own sheep by name."

Most of us are totally unaware of just how well God really does know us. We are oblivious to the staggering truth that every aspect of our lives is fully known to Him. If we examine the Word of God on this subject we will discover that even from our conception in our mother's womb all the hereditary factors that combined to make us each the unique individuals that we are have been known to God.

A careful reading of Psalm 139 assures us that we are known far beyond human knowledge, even in the environmental influences that have shaped us, by God who comprehends our complexities. All the multitudinous idiosyncrasies which make each of us distinct individuals are known to our Lord and Master.

The Good Shepherd may well be a stranger to me, but I am no stranger to Him!

When in the process of time an individual opens the sheepfold of his life to Christ, he may feel he is inviting a stranger to enter. Yet the truth is that He who enters is not a stranger at all but the One who has in fact known us from before birth.

This discovery is really double-pronged. It is at the same time both reassuring, yet also alarming. It is wonderful to realize that at last there is someone who does know and understand me. If I have been the type of person who has played games with others and pulled the wool over their eyes, I will find I can't do it with God.

The hypocrisy has to end. I must begin to be open and honest with Him who knows me through and through—who calls me by name.

In calling to his sheep, the shepherd desires to lead them out of the sheepfold. Sheepfolds, especially in the East, are not pretty places. Their names may sound picturesque and romantic, but the enclosure where the sheep spend the night usually is an appalling spot.

Within the enclosing walls of stone, timber, bricks, or brush there is a continual build-up of dirt, debris, and dung. Not a blade of grass survives the eternal tramping of a thousand hooves. And as the seasons come and go the sheepfold lies ever deeper in its accumulated dung. The odors can be atrocious after rain and vile in the heat of the summer sun.

The good shepherd is up early at break of day to fling open the gate and lead his sheep out into fresh pastures and green grasslands. He will not allow his flock to linger within the corral for an hour longer than is necessary. There they can only stand still in the scorching sun or lie down to try and rest in the dirt and dung that clings to their coats and matts in their wool.

Gently the shepherd stands at the gate and calls to his own to come outside. As each animal passes him he calls it by name, examines it with his knowing eye, and, if necessary, searches with knowing hands beneath its coat, to see if all is well. It is a moving interlude at the dawn of each new day: a time of close and intimate contact between the owner and his flock.

The parallel in our own lives is not difficult to discover. It is in the little circle of our own constricted living that most of us feel most secure, most relaxed and perhaps most familiar.

But our great Good Shepherd calls us to come out of the restricted, petty round of our cramped lives. He wishes to lead us out into fresh new pastures and broad fields, perhaps to new places we have never been before.

The surprising thing is that many of us are not aware of just how drab, soiled, and dusty with accumulated debris our lives really are. We keep milling about in our same little circle. We are totally preoccupied with our self-centered interests. We go around and around, sometimes stirring up quite a dust, but never really accomplishing anything worthwhile. Our lives are cramped, selfish, and plagued with petty pursuits.

The tragedy of all this is that it can apply to every aspect of our lives. It can be true in a physical dimension where we allow ourselves to be cramped within four small walls or within the narrow confines of a city house or apartment. We can be cramped, too, in abused and neglected bodies.

We can likewise find ourselves corralled in a moral and mental dimension. We will not move out into new areas which enlarge the horizons of our minds or new experiences that stir and challenge our souls. We cringe from new vistas and fresh pursuits that will get us off the barren ground of our familiar old style.

Equally so is there a sense in our spiritual lives where God by His gracious Spirit calls us from and leads us out of our cramped experiences. He invites us to move out into the rich, nourishing pastures of His Word. He wants us to roam abroad in the wide ranges of new relationships with others of His flock. He longs to lead us beside still waters; in paths of righteousness; up into the exhilarating high country of the summer ranges where we are in close communion with Him.

The intentions He has for us are all good. His desires and aspirations for us are enormous, full of potential for unimagined benefit to us and others. Because the thoughts He thinks toward us are thoughts of peace and blessing, let us not hold back! It is the truly wise one who will allow himself to be led out into the broad fields of God's gracious blessings and benefits.

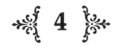

4

The Shepherd Puts Forth His Sheep

And when he putteth forth his own sheep, he goeth before them. (John 10:4a)

AS WAS POINTED out in the preceding chapter many sheepfolds are polluted places. Even the environs around the sheepfold often become barren, trampled, and eroded by the passing to and fro of the flock. So if they are to benefit from the outlying fields and meadows they must be put out to pasture.

A good shepherd simply does not permit his stock to linger long on the barren, contaminated ground around the corral. There is nothing of value there for them to feed upon. The corral is essentially a place of protection during darkness.

The diligent owner will be up at dawn to put his flock afield. This is a self-imposed discipline. He must bestir himself before the sun breaks over the eastern skyline, but this he does gladly and willingly for the sake of his sheep.

A reason for this is that because of the aridity of so much sheep country, he simply must get them out on grass early to benefit from the dew that lies on the herbage at dawn. Often this is the only moisture available for the flock. Frequently in these semi-desert countries there are no clear running streams nor placid pools of water where they can be refreshed. The total moisture intake to maintain body metabolism and vigor must come from dew-drenched vegetation.

Another point of interest is that this is the coolest time of the day. The atmosphere is moist and fragrant with the night air that has settled over the land. The heat has mostly dissipated during darkness. Mosquitoes, flies, and other insects are semidormant, less active, allowing the sheep to graze peacefully.

Turning to our lives we find that much the same principles hold true in our quiet times with the Master. It is noteworthy that most of the truly great men and women of God through the centuries are those who have met with Him early in the day. It is significant that so many of His most intimate "saints" have been those who literally allowed themselves to be "put out" into fresh fields of intimate association with Christ at break of day.

It is in these still hours that the quiet dews and refreshing presence of God's gracious Spirit descend upon us. It is then that the frantic world is still. It is then that the clamor and conflicts of our complex lives are quieted. It is then that we sense our own spirits can best be silent, responsive, and sensitive to the stimulus of His own strong Spirit.

Our Shepherd, our Lord, our Master Himself, when He was here among us as a man, delighted in these quiet hours in communion with His Father. The gospel record confirms how often He slipped away to be alone in private prayer and meditation. It was the time of refreshment for His soul; the time of restoration for His body and uplift for His spirit.

It is not always easy to be up and alert at an early hour. It demands a degree of self-discipline which is more than many can meet. But it is the interlude of enormous benefit to those who will allow themselves to be "put out" to this extent. So often, especially when we are weary, the comfort of our warm beds is so appealing. The natural, normal inclination is to simply sleep on.

> Yet a little sleep, a little slumber, a little folding of the hands to sleep: So shall thy poverty come as one that travelleth, and thy want as an armed man.
> (Prov. 6:10-11; 24:33-34)

The impoverishment which comes to us is often much greater than we recognize. Not only is it in a spiritual dimension, but it is equally so in mind and body. The reason for saying this is because the early hours are among the best of the day. It is then we are rested. Our minds are alert; our bodies are refreshed; our spirits are still. We are fully prepared for whatever new and fresh experience our Lord may have in mind for us. And if we deprive ourselves of this opportunity for a firsthand encounter with the living God, then our total lives are at a lower level than they could or should be.

It is the alert person who in a positive and distinct way presents himself or herself at dawn to the great Shepherd of the soul, who flourishes under God's care. In a dramatic way the course of the entire day's events are established. A strong, pervading, impelling awareness of God settles over us. We become acutely aware that we are, by a decisive action of our wills, putting ourselves at His disposal, to be put where He wishes during the day. We realize that we are going out into the turmoil of our times; into the chaos of our society; into the broken world of our generation, *not alone but with Him.*

It is because of this knowledge, this awareness, that, as God's people, we can be put out into a troubled generation with strength, serenity, and stability. It is He who puts us into the place of His appointment. It is He who will put us into the green pastures of His choosing. It is He who will make even our most desperate days of benefit to a beleaguered world. This He will do even to the refreshing of our own lives.

Why then, it may be asked, are so many of us reluctant to be put out of our little lives? Why are we so loathe to have our life habits disturbed? Why are we so unwilling to be put out either for the benefit of ourselves or the welfare of others—including our Master Himself?

The answer is rather startling, yet simple. It is largely because most of us are stubborn and selfish. We find it much easier and more comfortable to confine ourselves to the familiar little round of our old self-centered lives. We are so enfolded with the comforts and conveniences that have conditioned our existence that we are reluctant to have our constricted circle of living disturbed. Our days may be drab and dry, as barren as any eastern sheepfold with its dust, dung, and debris, but we will not be put out of it.

Some dear souls are fully aware that this is so. In a way they come to almost abhor their own dry existence. But instead of allowing themselves to be put out they turn inward to indulge in endless self-pity and boredom.

Somehow they feel it is no fault of their own that they are caught in a confining little circle of hopelessly selfish living. They are so preoccupied with their own petty interests that the idea of being drawn out to new fields and fresh experiences is both unwelcome and frightening.

They have ears, yet they are deaf to the pleas of perishing people around them. They have eyes, yet they cannot see the broken humanity, homes, and hearts all about them. They have spirits, yet they are shriveled, shrunken, and atrophied with self-interest, unable to sense the needs and heart hunger of a sick society, a world groaning in despair.

To such our Great Shepherd comes, intending to put them out where they can count for something substantial in His economy.

Let us look at this whole concept in a practical and simple way. Let us remind ourselves that because our God has been all over the ground before He knows what He is doing with us. He does not put us out into places or experiences where we are caught in a crisis. There are no crises with Christ. He has all foreknowledge. He is totally familiar with every circumstance that will or can confront us.

It follows then that wherever He chooses to put us it is for Him familiar ground. We are not going out blind. We are setting out under His guidance. Our confidence is in His faithfulness to find the places where not only we, but also He and others will benefit most from our just being there. It is not a case of relying on our wits, intelligence, or insight. Rather, it is a question of unquestioned reliance on His utter reliability to put us into the right place at the right time in the right way. Because He is all-knowing and all-understanding and totally trustworthy we can depend fully on His faithfulness to do that which is best.

Now this applies to every aspect of our lives. In no way is it or can it be confined to just our spiritual experiences. With God, every aspect of life is totally sacred the moment He touches it. There is no distinction in the mind of God, as there is in ours, between secular and sacred when He has dynamic part in it. He desires that the total round of our little lives be lifted out of the mundane round of impoverished days, to the lofty and broad sweep of living to our fullest capacity under His control. He wants to broaden our horizons.

This is true because He declared unequivocally, "I am come that they might have life, and that they might have it more abundantly" (John 10:10).

What does this involve in basic terms? In Christian thinking there is too often a tendency to deal in abstract values and intangible ideas. Let us get down to basic human behavior. Perhaps we can begin with our bodies, our physical makeup.

If in truth I am God's person; if Christ has in fact entered my life, my body belongs to Him: He resides there. My right to do with it as I choose has been abdicated. It is now the residence of His gracious Spirit who is entitled to be sovereign in its conduct and care. I no longer have any right to misuse or abuse it. It is not to be overworked, overstressed, overfed, overindulged with drink, nor overcharged with sex.

As the sheep of Christ's care this body is to be under His management. It is to be put out of the confining, restricting, damaging environment of just four walls and cramped quarters. It is to be exposed fully and freely to the benefits of fresh air, sunshine, clean water, wholesome food, moderate exercise, and adquate sleep. These are provisions made for it by God. I should be willing to be put out to see they are met. This will benefit not only myself, but also my family, friends, and anyone else who encounters this healthy, wholesome, energetic, vigorous person.

Turning to my soul with its mind, emotions, and will, precisely the same principle applies. This is my person, now indwelt by the living Spirit of the living God. I shall not permit it to be cramped and contaminated by exposing it to such dusty trivia as newspaper propaganda, pornography, cheap debasing literature, hours of low caliber television programs, or rubbish from the mass media.

Instead, God's Spirit will lead me to expose myself to the finest in art, literature, and music. He will put me into situations where my mind can be improved and my soul can be stimulated with that which is beautiful and noble and lofty. I can and will become a person of broad interests, noble aspirations, and enormous enthusiasm because I belong to Him and He wishes to put me out into wide fields of fruitful and useful endeavor to benefit my generation.

The same is true in the realm of my spirit, where I commune with Him. In the deep intuition of my innermost being where I "know him," Christ comes to enlarge my life and the understanding of His will.

He leads me to browse widely and ruminate richly in His Word. He puts me out to touch a hundred or a thousand other lives by His direction. He enriches my fellowship and contact with those outside the little circle of my sheepfold. In short, because He does all this it is possible to make an impact on my generation out of all proportion to my one little life—because He is in it with me.

5

The
Sheep
Follow

. . . and the sheep follow him: for they know his voice. (John 10:4b)

IN CHAPTER 3 we learned how the sheep come to recognize their shepherd's voice and respond by running when called. Over a prolonged period of time they become acutely aware that it is always in their best interests to do this. They have learned to trust it, to rely on it, but even more significant, to actually enjoy hearing it.

This is simply because the voice and the shepherd are as one. His voice denotes his presence. His voice indicates he is there in person. His voice represents his power, authority, and ability to protect them in danger while also providing for their every need.

In essence the sheep become so acquainted with that voice that they know it intimately. They come to expect it. That voice of that owner speaks peace and plenty to them. To hear and know that voice is to be constantly reassured of the shepherd's care for them. It is evidence of his affection and faithfulness to them.

Precisely the same can apply to the Christian under Christ's control. His voice is not something we shrink from. It does not disturb or dismay us. We do not find it troubles us when He speaks.

We also learn to delight in hearing Him. We look forward to having Him speak to us. We enjoy the increasing awareness of His presence; we relish the individual interest He shows in us; we revel in the close intimacy of communion with Him. We delight in knowing assuredly that He has come to be with us and we can be with Him, ready and eager to follow Him.

Nowhere is there stress or strain in this relationship with the Shepherd of my soul. Its keeping has been deliberately entrusted to Him. A calm, strong, quiet assurance pervades me that in His care all is well. Absent from this commitment of myself to Him is any fear or foreboding. *I know Him. I know His voice. I know all is well.*

And this knowing applies to all of my life. It embraces not only the past and the present but applies equally to the unknown tomorrows. My days need not be charged with anxiety: There is no need to inject unnecessary stress into my sojourn of this day. He is here. His voice speaks strength, serenity, and stability to my soul.

So where He leads me I will follow!

Etched indelibly upon the walls of my memory is one tropical night when all alone, with no one near but

God Himself, I went out to walk softly beneath the rustling palms beside the Pacific Ocean. My life, it seemed, had reached an absolute impasse. There seemed no point to pushing on. Everything had ground to a deadly standstill. The future looked forbidding; in fact, it appeared positively hopeless.

From the depth of my being I cried out to Christ. Like a lost sheep bleating in desperation from the thicket in which it was stuck fast, I longed to hear my Shepherd's voice. He did not disappoint me!

He heard. He came. He called. He spoke. And in His voice that night, speaking to me clearly, distinctly through His Word, by His Spirit, my soul was reassured. I could hear Him say, "Entrust the keeping of your soul and life to Me. Let Me lead you gently in the paths of righteousness and peace. My part is to show the way. Your part is to walk in it. All will be well!"

It was so. And it has been to this day.

The question in all of this is, "Do I really *want* to follow Him? Do I really *want* to do His will? Do I *want* to be led?"

Some of us say we do without really meaning it. More than anything else it is like a sentimental wish. It is a half-hearted hope. It is a pleasant idea we indulge in during our better moments. Yet, too often deep down in our wills we still determine to do our own thing and go our own wayward ways.

It is precisely at this point where we come to grief in our walk with God. It is presumption of the worst sort to claim His commitments to us, made so freely and in such generosity, while at the same time refusing to comply with His commands or wishes because of our own inherent selfish desires.

Whatever else happens there remains this one, basic

fundamental fact that only the person *who wants to follow* Christ will ever do so. All the rest will become strays.

This word "follow" as used by our Lord implies much more than just the thought of sheep tagging along blindly behind their owner. It has within it the connotation of one who deliberately decides to comply with specific instructions.

For example, if one purchases a complicated clock or other piece of equipment that is to be assembled, along with it will come a sheet of instructions. At the top will be printed in large bold letters, "THESE DIRECTIONS MUST BE FOLLOWED." In other words, there can be no guarantee that it will work unless the directions are complied with and carried out to the minutest detail.

It is the same in carrying out God's commands. His clear instructions for our conduct and character have been laid out for us in His Word and in the life of our Lord, the Word enfleshed. There rests with us then the obligation to comply. As we cooperate and follow through we will find ourselves progressing. New areas of life, exciting experiences of adventure with Him will emerge as we move onto fresh ground. I quote here from *A Shepherd Looks at Psalm 23:* "As mentioned earlier it is no mere whim on God's part to call us sheep. Our behavior patterns and life habits are so much like that of sheep it is well nigh embarrassing."

First of all, Scripture points out the fact that most of us are a haughty and stubborn lot. We prefer to follow our own fancies and turn to our own ways. "All we like sheep have gone astray; we have turned every one to his own way" (Isa. 53:6). And this we do deliberately, repeatedly, even to our own disadvantage. There is something almost terrifying about the destructive self-determination of a human being. It is inexorably interlocked with personal pride and self-assertion. We insist we know what is best for us even though the disastrous results may be self-evident.

Just as sheep will blindly, habitually, stupidly follow one another along the same little trails until they become ruts that erode into gigantic gullies, so we humans cling to the same habits that we have seen ruin other lives.

Turning to "my own way" simply means doing what I want. It implies that I feel free to assert my own wishes and carry out my own ideas. And this I do in spite of every warning.

We read in Proverbs 14:12 and 16:25, "There is a way which seemeth right unto a man, *but* the end thereof are the ways of death."

In contrast to this, Christ the Good Shepherd comes gently and says, "I am the way, the truth, and the life: no man cometh unto the Father, but by me" (John 14:6). "I am come that they might have life, and that they might have it more abundantly" (John 10:10).

The difficult point is that most of us don't want to come. We don't want to follow. We don't want to be led in the paths of righteousness. Somehow it goes against our grain. We actually prefer to turn to our own way even though it may take us into trouble.

The stubborn, proud, self-sufficient sheep that persists in pursuing its old paths and grazing on its old polluted ground will end up a bag of bones on ruined land. The world we live in is full of such people. Broken homes, broken hearts, derelict lives, and twisted personalities remind us everywhere of men and women who have gone their own way. We have a sick society struggling to survive on beleaguered land. The greed and selfishness of mankind leaves behind a legacy of ruin and remorse.

Amid all this chaos and confusion Christ the Good Shepherd comes and says, "If any man will follow me, let him deny himself, and take up his cross, and follow me" (Matt 16:24). But most of us, even as Christians, simply don't want to do this. We don't want to deny ourselves, give up our right to make our own decisions. We don't want to follow; we don't want to be led.

Of course, most of us, if confronted with this charge, would deny it. We would assert vehemently that we are "led of the Lord." We would insist that we follow wherever He leads. We sing hymns to this effect and give mental assent to the idea. But as far as actually being led in paths of righteousness is concerned, precious few of us follow that path.

Actually this is the pivot point on which a Christian either "goes on" with God or at which point he "goes back" from following on.

There are many willful, wayward, indifferent Christians who cannot really be classified as followers of Christ. There are relatively few diligent disciples who forsake all to follow the Master.

Jesus never made light of the cost involved in following Him. In fact, He made it painfully clear that it was a rugged life of rigid self-denial. It entailed a whole new set of attitudes. It was not the natural, normal way a person would ordinarily live, and this is what made the price so prohibitive to most people.

In brief, seven fresh attitudes have to be acquired. They are the equivalent of progressive forward movements onto new ground with God. If one follows them he will discover fresh pasturage, new, abundant life, and increased health, wholesomeness, and holiness, in his walk with God. Nothing will please Him more, and certainly no other activity on our part can or will result in as great benefit to lives around us.

1) Instead of loving myself most I am willing to love Christ best and others more than myself.

Now love in a scriptural sense is not a soft, sentimental emotion. It is a deliberate act of my will. It means that I am willing to lay down my life, put myself out on behalf of another. This is precisely what God did for us in Christ. "Hereby perceive (understand) we the love of God, because he laid down his life for us" (1 John 3:16).

The moment I deliberately do something definite either for God or others that costs me something, I am expressing love. Love is "selflessness" or "self-sacrifice" in contradistinction to "selfishness." Most of us know little of living like this, or being "led" in this right way. But once a person discovers the delight of doing something for others, he has started through the gate which leads into one of God's green pastures.

2) Instead of being one of the crowd I am willing to be singled out, set apart from the gang.

Most of us, like sheep, are pretty gregarious. We want to belong. We don't want to be different in a big way, though we may wish to be different in minor details that appeal to our selfish egos.

But Christ pointed out that only a few would find His way acceptable, and to be marked as one of His would mean a certain amount of criticism and sarcasm from a cynical society. Many of us don't want this. Just as He was a man of sorrows and acquainted with grief, so we may be. Instead of adding to the sorrows and sadness of society we may be called on to help bear some of the burdens of others, to enter into the suffering of others. Are we ready to do this?

3) Instead of insisting on my rights I am willing to forego them in favor of others.

Basically this is what the Master meant by denying one's self. It is not easy nor natural to do this. Even in the loving atmosphere of the home, self-assertion is evident and the powerful exercise of individual rights is always apparent.

But the person who is willing to pocket his pride, to take a back seat, to play second fiddle without a feeling of being abused or put upon, has gone a long way onto new ground with God.

There is a tremendous emancipation from "self" in this attitude. One is set free from the shackles of personal pride. It's pretty hard to hurt such a person. He who has no sense of self-importance cannot be offended or deflated. Somehow such people enjoy a wholesome outlook of carefree abandon that makes their Christian lives contagious with contentment and gaiety.

4) Instead of being "boss" I am willing to be at the bottom of the heap. Or to use sheep terminology, instead of being "Top Ram" I'm willing to be a "tail-ender."

When the desire for self-assertion and self-aggrandizement gives way to the desire for simply pleasing God and others, much of the fret and strain is drained away from daily living.

A hallmark of the serene soul is the absence of "drive," at least drive for self-determination. The person who is prepared to put his personal life and affairs in the Master's hands for His management and direction has found the place of rest in fresh fields each day. These are the ones who find time and energy to please others.

5) Instead of finding fault with life and always asking: Why? I am willing to accept every circumstance of life in an attitude of gratitude.

Humans, being what they are, somehow feel entitled to question the reasons for everything that happens to them. In many instances life itself becomes a continuous criticism and dissection of one's circumstances and acquaintances. We look for someone or something on which to pin the blame for our misfortunes. We are often quick to forget our blessings, slow to forget our misfortunes.

But if one really believes his affairs are in God's hands, every event, no matter whether joyous or tragic, will be taken as part of God's plan. To know beyond doubt that He does all for our welfare is to be led into a wide area of peace and quietness and strength for every situation.

6) Instead of exercising and asserting my will, I learn to cooperate with His wishes and comply with His will.

It must be noted that all the steps outlined here involve the will. The saints from earliest times have repeatedly pointed out that nine-tenths of being a Christian, of becoming a true follower, a dedicated disciple, lies in the will.

When a man allows his will to be crossed out, canceling the great "I" in his decision, then indeed the Cross has been applied to that life. This is the meaning of taking up one's cross daily—to go to one's death—no longer my will in the matter but His will be done.

7) Instead of choosing my own way I am willing to choose to follow in Christ's way, simply to do what He asks me to do.

This basically is simple, straightforward obedience. It means I do what He asks me to do. I go where He invites me to go. I say what He instructs me to say. I act and react in the manner He maintains is in my best interest as well as for His reputation.

Most of us possess a formidable amount of factual information on what the Master expects of us. Precious few have either the will, intention, or determination to act on it and comply with His instructions. But the person who decides to do what God asks him has moved onto fresh ground which will do both him and others a world of good. Besides, it will please the Good Shepherd.

God wants us all to move on with Him. He wants us to walk with Him. He wants it not only for our welfare but for the benefit of others as well as His own reputation.

Perhaps there are those who think He expects too much of us. Maybe they feel the demands are too drastic. Some may consider His call impossible to carry out.

It would be if we had to depend on self-determination or self-discipline to succeed. But if we are in earnest about wanting to do His will, and to be led, He *makes this possible* by His own gracious Spirit who is given to those who obey (Acts 5:32). For it is He who works in us "both to will and to do of his good pleasure" (Phil. 2:13).

❧ 6 ❧
A Stranger Will They Not Follow

And a stranger will they not follow, but will flee from him: for they know not the voice of strangers. (John 10:5)

AFTER LONG AND intimate association sheep become beautifully adjusted to their owner. They develop a touching and implicit trust in him and only in him. Wherever he takes them they simply "tag along" without hesitation. In quiet and uncomplaining reliance upon him they accompany him anywhere he goes. In his company they are contented and at rest.

This can be equally true in our Christian experience. Unfortunately for many of us it is not always so. Despite the tendency not to trust ourselves completely to Christ, there are those occasional times when we have.

Almost all of us have known what a stimulating delight it has been to respond to the Master's voice, to run to do His will, and thus discover His remarkable provision for us. We call this living or walking by faith.

Because the world is so much with us and we are so much in the world, our responses to Christ are not always as acute as they could be. Because from early childhood we have been conditioned to materialistic or humanistic or scientific concepts, it is not always easy to distinguish God's voice from the many other voices calling to us from the contemporary world. Because we have been taught and trained to be busy, active, energetic individuals, the main thrust of our times is to be people "on the go." This is true even if we really don't have any clear idea where we are going or what our ultimate destination may be.

Modern man is often a frustrated, frantic, fearful person racing madly on his own man-made treadmill.

This is not just true of the twentieth-century western world. It has ever been thus in the history of our race. It matters not whether an individual's life is spent in the feverish, high-pressure atmosphere of a modern executive office in Manhattan or in the feverish, humid, swamplands of the Amazon basin where a primitive hunter struggles to survive. All men know something of the unremitting, unrelenting fever of living.

And to all of us Christ comes with His incredible call, "Come unto me, all ye that labour and are heavy laden, and I will give you rest" (Matt. 11:28).

This invitation is not one to lethargy or indolence. It is not a formula for opting out of life. It is rather the delightful way of walking through the tangled turmoil of our times in quiet company with Christ.

To put this down on paper is fairly simple. To put it into daily practice is much more demanding and difficult. The reason I say this is simply because it is not just Christ who calls us to Himself. It is not just the Good Shepherd who invites us to walk with Him in the paths of right living and right relationships. It is not just the One who loves us deeply and desires our companionship who would have us follow Him.

There are scores of foreign influences appealing to us. On every side there are false pretenders to our ownership. We are sometimes surrounded by counterfeit "shepherds" who would have us believe they have our best interests at heart. When, in reality, they are predators disguised in various cloaks of respectability bent on our destruction. In some cases they are already among us, parading themselves as one of our own, while at the same time plotting our ruin.

In the Scriptures they have been given various names. In the Old Testament they are referred to frequently as "the shepherds which feed themselves and not the flock." Our Lord called them "false prophets" or "wolves in sheep's clothing." Elsewhere they are called "dogs" who devour the sheep.

In some cases these "strangers" have occupied places of prominence in our society. They may be preachers, teachers, writers, lecturers, broadcasters, or people of great influence posing as our protectors. Some may well go beyond even this and parade themselves as "saviours" to their fellowmen. They invite their contemporaries to come along with them and follow in their footsteps.

To a much lesser degree, but just as dangerous, are those common people who in their own quiet, subtle way insinuate themselves into our intimate circle of companions. They may be members of our family, among our friends, in the societies we join, in our business world, amid professional people, or even in the church.

It requires constant alertness on our part not to be victimized by imposters. We simply cannot afford to follow strangers if we are to survive as contented Christians who are attuned only to the call of our Master.

It may seem to the reader that this point is being unduly labored here. But the simple fact is that it is literally impossible to live in serenity of soul if we are torn between trying to follow conflicting calls at the same time. Our Lord was blunt about this. He stated emphatically, "No man can serve two masters: for either he will hate the one, and love the other; or else he will hold to the one, and despise (ignore) the other" (Matt. 6:24).

Too many of us have tried too long to make the best of both worlds. We have tried to live with one foot following Christ and the other following the false ideas and teachings of our times.

And the plain position which the Good Shepherd takes is a simple one: "My sheep—those who *know* Me—simply will not follow strangers." How easy it sounds; how difficult to do!

It is, of course, outside the scope of this book to list or even enumerate the false ideologies, misleading concepts, damaging philosophies, and strange teachings which are so much a part of the contemporary scene. They proliferate on every side. They are spewed out in floods of printed matter, in radio broadcasts and television shows that now engulf the entire planet—to say nothing of the person to person contacts.

But broadly all of these strange and false concepts are based on the following themes.

1) Humanism. Man is master of his own destiny. He is the supreme being in the universe. There is no superior power or intelligence to which he need appeal.

2) Materialism. The chief end of life is the attainment and acquisition of tangible values. The measure of a man's success is not the quality of his character but the quantity of things he has accumulated, or knowledge (human) he has acquired.

3) Scientism. Only that which can be subjected to the scientific method of examination is real. It must be evaluated empirically on the basis of our five fallible finite senses. Any dimension of divinity or deity is ruled out as invalid.

4) Atheism. Insists that there cannot be such a Being as God. All that exists does so by pure chance. Existence which is evolutionary has neither purpose nor meaning nor direction.

5) Religionism. Man's blind, unguided groping after God. The wild guessing at what God may be like. An abortive attempt to interpret the character and conduct of God from the distorted viewpoint of man still in the darkness of his own sin and despair.

6) Spiritism. All of the occult, including demonism and satanic emulation. This includes all aspects of contact with the realm of evil spirits in opposition to God our Father, God the Son, Jesus Christ, and God the Holy Spirit.

7) Higher Criticism. In Christian circles it denies: the authenticity of God's Word, the deity of Christ, the necessity for the redemption and reconciliation of sinful men to a loving God.

If and when we detect these notes sounding in the voices which call to us as Christians we should be on guard at once. Paul, with his brilliant intellect, broad background of education, and enormous spiritual perception warned the church at Colossae. "Beware lest any man spoil you through philosophy and vain deceit, after the tradition of men, after the rudiments of the world, and *not after Christ*" (Col. 2:8).

Apart from the falsity of strange and unfamiliar teaching there is a second way in which God's people can reassure themselves that these imposters are in fact false shepherds. That is by the actual character and conduct of their lives.

Invariably a man or woman lives what he or she truly believes. Our life style is an unconscious reflection of our inner convictions, and inevitably it will be found that the behavior pattern of the "false shepherds"— "false prophets"—"wolves in sheep's clothing" will be a dead giveaway as to who they really are.

Put in the language of Scripture we say, "By their fruits ye shall know them." No matter how smooth, subtle, or reassuring their words or manner may be, ultimately it is the quality of their lives which will declare their true identity.

As Christians we are wise to not only examine carefully the content of the voice we are called by, but also the character of the one who calls to us. A person's words may drip with honey but be potent poison coming from a corrupt conscience.

It is true we may be likened to sheep because of our mob instincts. But we need not be always ignorant, dumb sheep. If we have heard and known the delight in our Shepherd's voice; if we revel and rejoice in His companionship, we are worse than fools if we do not flee from strangers to Him.

Sheep are among the most timid and helpless of all livestock. Though they will often hammer and batter each other, both rams and ewes, they will run in panic from the least threat of unknown danger. I have seen an entire flock rush away in blind fear simply because one of them was startled by a rabbit bursting out from beneath a bush.

Yet, in a peculiar manner they will sometimes stand still and stare blankly when a powerful predator comes among them. They will huddle up in tight, frightened little knots, watching dumbly while one after another of the flock is torn to pieces by the wolf, bear, leopard, cougar, or dog that may be ravaging them, or similarly they may be stolen by rustlers.

The only sheep that have any chance to escape are those that flee for their lives. They must get out of danger. There is simply no other hope of survival. Somehow they must separate themselves from the attacker who would destroy them.

Our Lord knew all this. He was thoroughly familiar with the hazards of sheep management. No doubt many of the shepherds who had come to His carpenter's shop in Nazareth to have Him build tables and benches for their humble homes had regaled Him with tales about the terrible losses they suffered from predators and rustlers.

This is one of the favorite topics of conversation for

sheep men. And always, in the end, they know that the only place of safe protection for the sheep is close to the shepherd himself, within earshot of his voice.

The voice that is such an assurance to them is at the same time a terror to their enemies. That voice, which speaks of safety and well-being in the Master's care, instills fear and respect in the raiders.

To thrive and flourish, the sheep have to be ever under the sound of that familiar, friendly voice. To be allured away or distracted by any other is to face utter destruction or complete loss.

When I was an impressionable young man, one of the jobs given to me was to paint a huge building. At that time, because of a tempestuous boyhood and great adversity in my late teens, I was bitter and hostile toward society. My early life had been a tough struggle to survive amid severe hardships. So my mind was fertile ground for subversive ideas.

Working with me on the big barn, teaching me the tricks and skills of painting, was an old master craftsman. He was a Swede and an excellent painter. But he was also an ardent and avowed revolutionary. Day after day, sitting side by side high on the swing stage, he poured his subversive propaganda into my malleable mind.

It remains a miracle that my entire life was not destroyed by that invidious, crafty campaign. But some twelve thousand miles away, half way around the world, my dear mother, widowed and lonely, poured out her soul in tears that her wayward son would be spared from the snares and attacks of the enemy.

And one day, unable to endure the perverse propaganda poured into my ears by the old painter, I went to my boss and demanded another job where I could work alone. I wanted to be free. I wanted to flee from my foe. Something about that smooth, subtle voice of destruction alerted me to my mortal danger.

I give God thanks that other work was provided for me. It was possible to separate myself from the one who would have ruined me. To flee from a strange voice that brought foreign and damaging ideas was my only salvation.

Later in life, when my own children were teenagers, soon to leave home, I counseled them to do the same. Whenever they found themselves in the company of those who were not God's people, who were endeavoring to destroy them, there was one simple solution: "Just get out of there."

"The sheep will flee from strangers for they do not know their voice."

It is not weakness to do this. It is wisdom. Most of us, sad to say, simply are not skilled enough nor astute enough to match wits with our opponents. We are not sufficiently familiar, nor can we be, to fully understand or master all the devious and destructive devices of false philosophies, cults, religions, and ideologies of our modern world.

But what we can do is to become so grounded in God's Word, so familiar with our Master's voice, so attuned to His will and wishes, so accustomed to His presence, that any other voice alerts us to danger. It is a question of having our souls and spirits in harmony with His. It is a matter of living in close communion with the Shepherd of our lives. Then, and only then, will the threat of strange voices be recognized.

This does not mean that if I live in an environment or culture where one or two false philosophies predominate I am to remain ignorant of them. No, I will learn all about their insidious tactics to take God's people unawares. And in my alertness to their depredations I may well save both myself and others from their ravages.

Engaging the enemy in endless disputes and arguments seldom achieves anything. Paul was aware of this when he wrote to his young protege, Timothy. Over and over he advised him against becoming embroiled in unprofitable debates with those who posed pointless and false issues.

What Christ asks us to do as His followers is to concentrate on keeping close to Him. Our major distinctive as His disciples should be the unique life we have because of our intimate association with Him. He resides with us and in us. We likewise live with Him and in Him. Therein lies our strength, our serenity, our stability, and our safety. There is simply no substitute for this wondrous relationship with Him in a warped world.

His audience of that day, except for the young man born blind, and the young adulteress, whose lives He had entered, just could not understand what He said. Nor can most of our contemporaries.

PARABLE II

John 10:7-18

ME IN CHRIST

❧{ 7 }❧

The Doorway For the Sheep

Then said Jesus unto them again, Verily, verily, I say unto you, I am the door of the sheep. All that ever came before me are thieves and robbers: but the sheep did not hear them. (John 10:7-8)

IN THE FIRST parable of this intercourse, our Lord made clear what He meant when He spoke of entering into the fold of one's life. Now, in the second parable, He proceeds to elaborate in great detail what it means for a man or woman to enter into His life. By that is implied the way whereby we come into His care, enjoy His management, and revel in the abundance of His life shared with us in gracious generosity.

Again it must be emphasized that His audience did not really understand Him. When He completed His teaching they charged Him with being insane . . . possessed of an evil spirit, and unworthy of a hearing. And since that time millions of others have been bewildered by His teaching.

But the man born blind and the young woman taken in adultery, as well as a few others whose lives He had touched and transformed, understood Him. They knew it was God who had entered their lives. Also they had been introduced into a new life in Christ which was a dimension of living unknown to them before. These few grasped what it was He said.

Perhaps as we proceed to study His statements we, too, can enter into a fuller comprehension of the spiritual truths He shared with His audience. To do so is to have the horizons of our spiritual understanding widened by His words.

"I am the door of the sheep." Put into our modern idiom we would say: "I am the doorway, the entrance, for the sheep." Too often people have the wrong idea that our Lord referred to Himself only as the actual door or gate used to close a passageway into a sheepfold. This is not the picture.

The whole process of sheep management, of folding sheep, is combined with the control of doorways and gateways. It is by means of opening and shutting these passageways that the flock is moved methodically in and out, from place to place. They pass in through it to the protection of the fold within.

A flock has both an interior life within the shelter of the sheepfold and an exterior life outside. It is by means of the doorway, through the opening of the gate, that they enjoy both ingress and egress to a fully rounded and beneficial mode of life.

In the experience of every Christian whose life Christ has entered by His gracious Spirit, there are really two distinct areas of living. There is that inner life which the Quakers sometimes refer to as "the interior life." It is a personal, private, precious communion which a person enjoys within the inner sanctum of his own soul and spirit.

Then there is that outer life in which one is in contact with fellow Christians. It does not just end there, however, for it reaches out to touch all the world around us. This we refer to as our "exterior life," where thousands of contacts are made in a lifetime of interaction with our contemporaries.

The person under Christ's control will sense and know the hand of the Good Shepherd directing him in both areas. He will be acutely aware that it is through Him he passes in and out peacefully wherever He wishes us.

Whether it is within the stillness of our own spirits or without in the noisy world around us, He is there. This acute awareness of His presence opening or closing the way before me is a magnificent reassurance to my soul that all is well.

The doorway was of tremendous import in Hebrew tradition and thought; much more so than in our culture. It was against the background of the Hebrew respect for "the door" that Christ made this assertion repeatedly—"I am the door." We do well to examine this briefly in order to fully comprehend what He meant.

Early in her history as a nation, Israel had been enslaved by the Egyptians. For nearly two hundred years her people had been driven by their taskmasters to toil in the dreadful slime pits. There under the broiling sun they made mud bricks with which to build the great, elaborate cities of their enemies.

Though this subservient people lived in their own little peasant hovels by the Nile, they were still prisoners of their Egyptian lords. In desperation they cried out for deliverance. God responded to their cry and sent Moses to wrest them from the land of their bondage.

The final great act of their emancipation had to do with the door of each man's home. A spotless Passover Lamb was to be slaughtered for each household. Its blood was to be liberally sprinkled on the lintel over the door, and on both doorposts. Any person passing through this door to the shelter of the house within was assured of perfect protection and absolute safety from the awesome judgment of the great destroying angel who swept through Egypt in the darkness.

But also by the same door anyone going out entered into the magnificent exodus which was able to deliver the enslaved from their bondage. A person went out through that door to liberty, freedom, and a new dimension of life under God's direction (Exod. 1-15).

It was the blood of the innocent Passover lamb, applied to the owner's doorway, that guaranteed him peace within and protection without. He had come directly under God's care and control within a new life of freedom.

And so it is in the experience of any man or woman who complies with the provisions of Christ. As we come to rely implicitly upon the efficacy of His laid-down life and spilled blood on our behalf, He, God's own Passover Lamb, in very fact becomes the doorway for us. It is through Him that we enjoy a magnificent inner security and through Him that we go out to engage in an adventurous life of new-found freedom under His direction.

Later in the history of the nation Israel, clear and specific instructions were given regarding the doorway to a man's home. The great laws and commandments of God to His people were to be inscribed on long, thin strips of parchment. These were to be carefully wrapped around each of the doorposts through which a person passed in and out of his home. Thus the resident was continually reminded, as were any strangers or visitors who came to call on him, that he and his family lived and moved under the command and control of God. Their going out and their coming in from that time forth were under the guidance of God's Word (Deut. 11:18-21).

Again this was a beautiful concept clearly portraying to God's own people the fact that they were under His care. It was under His hand and under His gracious guidance that in truth they could live securely. As they passed their days going in and out of their humble homes it was to find sweet serenity within and strong safety without. Jehovah God was with them to guide. The Shepherd of their souls was their salvation in every situation.

We see this same remarkable theme and emphasis reiterated throughout the teachings of our Lord. He stated emphatically in His great Sermon on the Mount that the gateway or doorway through which anyone entered into an abundant life of new-found freedom was in truth a restricted one. One could not think that he could pursue any course he chose and still come out right. If he did this he would end up in disaster—a wayward, willful, lost sheep.

No, the way to safety within and security without was only through the gateway of the Good Shepherd's care. Not many would either find or follow that route.

Most preferred to go their own proud, perverse path to perdition.

Jesus the Christ was even more specific about this matter when, just before His crucifixion, He stated simply: "I am the way, the truth, and the life: no man cometh unto the Father, but by me" (John 14:6).

Putting this into plain language He is saying: "I am the way in and through which anyone can enter into a splendid new life with God. It is through Me that a man or woman comes to discover truth, reality, purpose, and meaning. It is through Me that one comes into the intimacy of the family of God our Father."

This is the main thrust of the entire New Testament. It is remarkable to see stated over and over the assertion that it is in and through Christ we live.

Through Jesus Christ I have peace with God.

Through Jesus Christ I am justified.

Through Jesus Christ I am forgiven my failures and sins.

Through Jesus Christ I am accepted into God's family.

Through Jesus Christ I am set free from slavery to sin and self.

Through Jesus Christ I am resurrected.

Through Jesus Christ I have immediate access to God in prayer.

And so the list could go on as a paean of praise to Him who has loved us and redeemed us and reconciled us to Himself by His own generous laid-down life.

In a word, it may be said that He, and only He, is the doorway into abundant living.

As in the previous parable, here again the Lord reiterates that anyone who ever preceded Him in our experience was a thief or robber. He was a thief in that if he induced us to do our own thing and go our own way he robbed us of our rightful inheritance.

The reason for this escapes most people. We are conditioned by the culture of our society to believe that we are in the world merely to gratify our own selfish desires and drives. We are taught that to a great degree everything is relative. If my impulse is to push my way to the top of the totem pole, I should do so, even if it means trampling on others along the way. It's just too bad if others are injured. After all, it's a tough world we live in, and life is really a struggle to survive.

So, little by little as time goes on, many of us do not believe that the standards established by God are relative to our age. We discard His directions for living. We ignore His instructions for our conduct. We turn each to his own way only to find our difficulties deepen. We see ourselves caught up in a worldly way of existence. Life becomes a meaningless mockery. God's absolute values of integrity, loyalty, justice, honor, love, and fine nobility are cast aside. And in their place we find ourselves an impoverished people left only with discouragement and despair. We are robbed blind and left destitute with broken lives, broken hearts, broken minds, broken homes, broken bodies, and a broken society.

Jesus was speaking a truth we should pay attention to when He said that it was possible for us to be pillaged and plundered by the false philosophies and crass materialism of our times. Unhappily most people simply won't believe Him. They know better, or so they think. But they end up broken and beaten.

There is a second, and even more subtle way in which we ignore Him as the "way" and put others "before Him." It has to do with our basic priorities.

Again it is helpful to go back into the early Hebrew teachings and traditions. The first of the Ten Commandments given by God to Moses in Exodus 20 states explicitly, "Thou shalt have no other gods before me!" God knew that to do so would spell certain disaster. No one, no thing, no human ideology could begin to compare with God Himself in wisdom, might, love, or integrity. In Him resided all that was selfless, noble, and glorious.

For us to give ourselves or our allegiance to any other is to impoverish and demean ourselves: it is never to know *the best.*

Yet, in our blindness, ignorance, and folly all through the long and tragic tale of human history men have sold themselves short to all sorts of strange and stupid gods. We have bartered away our birthright for a meager mess of unsatisfying substitutes.

God made us for Himself. In love and concern He intended us to be the children of His family, the sheep of His flock, the bride for His bridegroom.

Instead of seeing, longing, and devoting ourselves to Him, we have turned away and have put all sorts of other gods before Him. Other interests, ideas, people, and pursuits have been given prior place in our lives and affections. They have all "come before" Him.

Whatever it is to which I give most of my attention, time, thought, strength, and interest, becomes my God. It may be my home, my health, my family, career, hobby, entertainment, money, or person.

But our Lord says that if they come before Him, we are robbed. We have been stolen blind. We are poorer than we think. Our plight is pathetic, and we have settled for second best.

Our Lord points out in our text that those who are truly His people, the sheep of His pasture, will not allow themselves to be subverted by false gods. In the history of the people of Israel this had always been one of their greatest difficulties. Often they had been warned not to follow after the pagan gods of the races around them. Whenever they gave an ear to their subtle attractions they were drawn into dreadful practices that led them to utter ruin.

It did not matter whether they did this collectively as a nation or privately as individual citizens. The end result always was retrogression and remorse. But in spite of the repeated warnings there always seemed to be those who were oblivious to the dangers of thieves and robbers. In stubborn, sometimes blind folly they would fall prey to the predators among them or around them. And the same is still true today.

It reminds me of the behavior of a band of sheep under attack from dogs, cougars, bears, or even wolves. Often in blind fear or stupid unawareness they will stand rooted to the spot watching their companions being cut to shreds. The predator will pounce upon one then another of the flock raking and tearing them with tooth and claw. Meanwhile, the other sheep may act as if they did not even hear or recognize the carnage going on around them. It is as though they were totally oblivious to the obvious peril of their own precarious position.

We see this principle at work even among Christians. We as God's people are continually coming under attack, either from without or within. Yet many are unable to detect danger among our number. It is as though we cannot hear or see or sense our peril. Often the predation is so crafty and cunning that fellow

89

Christians are cut down before our eyes by the enemy of our souls.

Sometimes those who do the most damage are already among us. They insinuate themselves into our little folds. They may be in our family, among our friends, in our neighborhood, in some small Bible class, in the community, or even in the church itself. They come bringing discord, divisions, and dissension. They rob us of the enrichment we might have from our Master by redirecting our attention to lesser issues. We get caught up in conflict and confusion that can lead to chaos. Instead of our focus being centered on Christ they get us embroiled with false and destructive ideas that may eventually lead to our downfall.

Almost invariably those who come as thieves and robbers divert our attention from the loveliness and grandeur of our Good Shepherd. They manage to redirect our interests to peripheral issues of minor importance. They will get us to expend our time and energy and thought on trivia. And while we are so preoccupied with following their "will-o-the-wisp" suggestions we fall prey to their deceptive and destructive tactics. We see this in such things as overemphasis of questionable doctrines, humanistic philosophies, undue desire for feelings rather than faith in the Christian experience, disputes over biblical interpretations, excesses in legalism, worldly ways of living or doing God's work, pandering to certain popular personalities or programs.

Throughout the teachings of our Lord, and later in the writings of the New Testament apostles (see 2 Tim.), we are warned "not to hear" such false teachers. We are urged to turn a deaf ear to them. We are told to flee from them. If we are to survive we must disassociate ourselves from them. We do not respond to those who treacherously try to tickle our ears while cutting our throats.

This is not always easy to do, but if we are following Christ in an intimate communion, we will be aware of our danger. We will turn from those who would maim and mutilate us. We will be acutely sensitive only to the gentle voice of the Good Shepherd.

⚜ 8 ⚜
Entering Into
A
New Life

I am the door: by me if any man enter in, he shall be
saved, and shall go in and out, and find pasture. The
thief cometh not, but for to steal, and to kill, and to
destroy. (John 10:9-10a)

OUR LORD MAKES it clear that He is the door, the way,
the entrance into a new life. This life in which He
controls both my interior and exterior life is totally
different from any life style I may have known before.

It implies a new two-way interpersonal
relationship. He has come into the little
fold of my life there to exercise His management of my affairs. He leads me out in
due course to wider fields of contact and
adventure with others in new dimensions
of spiritual growth.

Yet, at the same time I find myself entering into an exciting and

stimulating life style within the *enfolding control* of His presence. He has become the paramount and preeminent person in my daily experience. He occupies a place of greater priority in my thoughts, emotions, and decisions than any earthly companion. This applies to my family, friends, or other intimate associates.

This process of gradually allowing God to govern my life, permitting Christ to control my conduct, coming gently under the absolute sovereignty of His gracious Spirit is to enter into the remarkable and restful salvation He provides for His people.

It is a case where I am no longer enslaved to my own small, self-centered wishes. I am set free from the tyranny of my own destructive emotions. I am liberated from the bondage of my own bungling decisions. It is a case of being set free from the terrible tyranny of my own selfish self-centeredness. He, the Good Shepherd of my soul, takes over the welfare of my affairs. He delivers me from the dilemma of my own self-destructive drives. I am free at last to enter into the joyous delight of just doing His will.

Sad as it may seem, many Christians do not enter into the rest and repose of this life in Christ. They may have heard about it. They may have read about it. They may even have seen it in the experience of one or two of their contemporaries, but for themselves it is as elusive as a passing daydream.

Perhaps if a parallel is drawn from the relationships between a shepherd and his sheep we can understand how one enters into this wondrous life.

Any sheep, if treated with kindness and affection, soon attaches itself to its new owner. Sheep are remarkably responsive, for the most part, to the attention and care given to them by a good shepherd. This is especially true in small flocks where the owner has opportunity to bestow his personal affection on individual animals. They quickly become his friends. A select few are actually pets. They follow him as faithfully as his own shadow. Wherever he goes they are there. It is in his company, and because of his presence, that they are ever secure and at rest.

The same truth applies in our relationship to Christ. We can in truth enter into a new life with Him whereby we enjoy the safety, surety, and security of His presence. This is not some superspiritual, once-for-all, ecstatic experience. Rather it is the quiet, gentle hour-to-hour awareness of "O Lord, You are here!" It is the keen knowledge, "O God, You are guiding me!" It is the calm, serene assurance, "O gracious Spirit, in Your presence there is peace!"

There is nothing mystical or magical about this. It is the winsome, wondrous knowledge of realizing the person, presence, and power of Christ in every detail of my day. This is the meaning of salvation in its full-orbed splendor.

The entering into this life in Christ lifts me above the low level of trying to struggle with the down-drag of sin that leads so many into the deep ditch of despair. It frees me from the fret of fighting with the old selfish impulses that generally govern my life. It delivers me from the dominion of the enemy of my soul who wishes to ensnare me.

The focus of my attention has been shifted away from myself to my Shepherd. The movement of my soul has been brought to Him for direction rather than left in the dilemma of my own decision making. The responsibility for my activities has been placed squarely in His care and taken out of my hands. This means subjecting my will to His wishes, but therein lies my rest and relief from my own stressful way of life.

Such people, our Lord said, would go in and out freely and find pasture.

Many people assume that to become a Christian and follow Christ calls only for self-denial, privation, poverty, and hardships. It is a distorted picture, for in fact, though we may relinquish our old selfish life style, we discover to our delight an entrance into a much greater and broader dimension of living.

Who is the person rich in friends, loved ones, and affection? The one willing to give himself away to others. Who is the individual who finds life full, rewarding, and deeply satisfying? The person who loses himself in a cause much greater than himself, who gives himself away for the greater good of all.

And it is to this caliber of life that Christ invites us. He calls us to enter into great commitments and noble causes. He leads us into a broken world there to expend ourselves on behalf of suffering, struggling, lost humanity.

Life is too magnificent, our capacities too noble, our days too few and precious to be squandered on just our own selfish little selves. God has made us in His own great image for great purposes. Only in coming into harmony with His will and wishes can we ever begin to realize or attain the tremendous aspirations He has for us. It is in complete and implicit cooperation with His ongoing purposes for the planet that any of us ever attain even a fraction of our potential for eternal service and salvation.

Too many of us are too provincial, too petty in our outlook. We see only our own little problems. We are obsessed with only our own little objectives. We go through life cramped and constricted by our own small circle of contacts.

Christ the Good Shepherd calls us to go in and out and find wide, broad pastures of practical and abundant service; not only for our own sakes but also for the sake of others who are as lost as we once were.

He gave us this broad view in graphic terms Himself when He sent out His twelve disciples as missionaries to the lost sheep of Israel.

A careful and intelligent reading of Matthew 9:35-10:16 discloses a delightful scene of an eastern shepherd gathering up stray sheep. Jesus had been moving from village to village, town to town, teaching, preaching, healing, and ministering to men's needs in every area of life. Seeing the innumerable multitudes of struggling souls He was moved with enormous concern and compassion for them. They were as sheep without a shepherd. They were weary, apprehensive, distraught, and scattered afield in every direction.

Turning to His twelve companions He made the comment, so often misunderstood and misinterpreted by missionaries. "The harvest truly is plenteous, but the labourers are few." He was not speaking of a harvest of wheat or corn or other grain, but rather a crop of lambs, a crop of lost sheep scattered by the millions, milling aimlessly across the surface of the earth.

Who and where were the workers, the laborers who could gather in the lost? There were so few able to do this difficult and delicate task.

How does an eastern sheepman gather up his stray sheep? How does He bring home the wanderers and stragglers?

He does not use dogs the way western sheepmen do.

He does not resort to horses or donkeys to herd them home or round them up. Nor does he employ helicopters or Hondas as some western ranchers do.

No, the eastern shepherd uses his own pet lambs and bellwethers to gather in lost sheep. Because these pets are so fond of being near him and with him, he has to literally go out into the hills and rough country himself taking them along, scattering them abroad. There they graze and feed alongside the wild and wayward sheep.

As evening approaches the shepherd gently winds his way home. His favorite pet lambs and bellwethers quietly follow him. As they move along in his footsteps, they bring with them the lost and scattered sheep. It is a winsome picture full of pathos.

In Matthew 10 Christ actually took His twelve men and scattered them out among the lost sheep of Israel (v. 6). He warned them that He was sending them out as sheep in the midst of predators who might try to prevent them from bringing home the lost (v. 16). But they were to go anyway, because the presence of His Spirit would be with them to preserve them in every danger.

This is a precise picture drawn for us in bold colors of what our Good Shepherd requires of us. He does not demand that we embark on some grandiose schemes of our own design to do His work in the world. He does not suggest that we become embroiled in some complex organization of human ingenuity to achieve His goal of gathering in lost souls.

He simply asks me to be one who will be so attached to Him, so fond of Him, so true to Him, that in truth I shall be like His pet lamb or bellwether. No matter where He takes me; no matter where He places me; no matter whom I am alongside of in my daily living, that person will be induced to eventually follow the Shepherd because I follow Him.

Put in another way it may be said that any Christian's effectiveness in winning others is directly proportional to his own devotion to the Master. Show me a person to whom Christ is absolutely paramount and I will show you one who gently but surely is gathering in others from the pastures of the world.

This is the individual who has entered into an exciting, adventuresome, fresh mode of life in God. Day after day, under the guidance of the Good Shepherd, he goes in and out to find fresh pastures of new experience. His life touches other lives, and all the time here and there he sees others gently gathered in, because he was willing to be sent forth wherever the Shepherd best saw fit to place him.

It all sounds fairly simple. It is, if we faithfully follow Christ. It is He who assures us of effective success in helping to save the lost and scattered sheep in a shattered world. We are His co-workers, colaborers in His great ongoing plans for rescuing the lost.

Nor is such labor without its rewards. Our God is the God of all consolation and compensation. He is no man's debtor. Those who honor Him, He will honor. If we put Him and His interests first, there will ever be ample provision for all of our needs. This is not theory. This is the truth testified to by uncounted millions of men and women who, having entered into this new life with God, have found Him to be ever faithful to them.

Any life He enters is always enriched, never impoverished. Any of our days He touches are transformed with the light and joy of His presence. To sense and know Him is to have tasted life at its sublime best.

Yet amid such living our Lord warns us that there can still be thieves and robbers present. There are always predators prowling around the periphery of our lives, waiting and watching for opportunity to plunder and impoverish us.

In previous chapters these have been dealt with in some detail. Emphasis has been placed especially upon those aspects of our Christian lives where we can be seriously endangered by false teaching, philosophies, or ideologies.

Here, very briefly, I would like to mention just two of the more practical aspects of our times which literally come into our lives and impoverish us. Not only are we poorer because of them, but God's work is hindered from being carried out as well as it might be.

The first is idleness. We live in a culture given to greater leisure. The shorter work week means more discipline of diligent duty is disappearing. Consequently the character of our people becomes increasingly casual, careless, and irresponsible.

For young people especially, excess ease is debilitating. The sense of challenge and achievement is lacking. They are impoverished because there is so little attained to satisfy them with a sense of worthwhile accomplishment. Too often the young toss away their days while the older loaf away their lives.

As God's people we should give ourselves completely, gladly, and wholeheartedly to His enterprises upon the earth. There is much to achieve!

Then there is affluence and luxury. The world is so much with us. We have been conditioned by our culture to believe that an individual's worth is measured by his material assets. Yet Christ declared, "A man's life does not consist of the abundance of things he owns" (Luke 12:15).

Still, there is a tendency for us to allow our attention to be centered on the acquisition of material wealth, or even academic attainments, or personal power and prestige in one form or another.

This is not to say that as Christians we are not entitled to pursue excellence in any of the fields into which God may guide us. We should strive to excel for His sake, not our personal pride. But at no time should these become a prior claim upon our thought or time or strength. If we allow this to happen we will soon discover that in truth we are being robbed of the best. We are being deprived of His presence, power, and peace in our lives. We will have settled for second best. We will be poorer than we know. This will constrict our effectiveness for Christ and will cramp our personal relationship to Him.

The Spirit of God speaking to the church of Laodicea in Revelation 3:16-20 put it this way:

> So then because thou art lukewarm, and neither cold nor hot, I will spue thee out of my mouth. Because thou sayest, I am rich, and increased with goods, and have need of nothing; and knowest not that thou art wretched, and miserable, and poor, and blind, and naked: I counsel thee to buy of me gold tried in the fire, that thou mayest be rich; and white raiment, that thou mayest be clothed, and that the shame of thy nakedness do not appear; and anoint thine eyes with eyesalve, that thou mayest see. As many as I love, I rebuke and chasten: be zealous therefore, and repent. Behold, I stand at the door, and knock: if any man hear my voice, and open the door, I will come in to him, and will sup with him, and he with me.

What the Good Shepherd desires above all else is that He might have the wondrous delight of entering *fully* into my life, there to share it with me. And I in turn can enter wholeheartedly into His great life, there to experience the remarkable fulfillment which He intended for me as His person. All of this is the purpose of His love for me.

❦ 9 ❧

The
Abundant Life

I am come that they might have life, and that they
might have it more abundantly. I am the good
shepherd: the good shepherd giveth his life for the
sheep. (John 10:10b-11)

ANY SHEPHERD WHO is a good manager always bears in
mind one great objective. It is that his flock may
flourish. The continuous well-being of his sheep is his
constant preoccupation. All of his time, thought, skill,
strength, and resources are directed to this end.

Nothing delights the good shepherd more than to
know his livestock are in excellent condition. He will
stand in his pastures amongst his sheep casting a
knowing eye over
them, rejoicing
in their con-

tentment and fitness. A good stock man actually revels in the joy of seeing his animals flourishing.

There are several reasons for this. First, and perhaps foremost, is the simple fact that sheep that are in good health are free from all the trying and annoying ailments of parasitism and disease that so frequently decimate sheep. He does not have to worry about sick or crippled animals. They are thriving under his care.

Second, it means that most of his time and attention can be devoted to the development and care of the entire ranch. This will assure his stock of an ideal environment in which they can prosper. He can supply abundant pasturage, clean water supplies, proper shelter, protection from predators, ample range, and ideal management in every area of the ranch operation.

This is the best guarantee that the flock in his ownership will derive maximum benefit from his expertise.

Third, his own reputation and name as an esteemed sheepman is reflected in the performance of his flock. All of his expertise and affection for the sheep is shown by how they prosper under his watchful eye. When they are thriving he also benefits. Not only does he prosper but he feels richly rewarded in soul for all his strength and life actually poured into them.

Put another way it may be said that the outpouring of his own being is to be seen in the excellence of his stock. It is very much a demonstration of the eternal principle that what a man gets out of life is what he puts into it.

Reflecting back over my own years as a sheepman I recall clearly those happy, contented times when I literally revelled in the well-being of my sheep. Visitors would often remark how contented and flourishing my flock appeared. But only I knew how much work, effort, tireless attention, and never-ending diligence had been expended on my part for this to be possible.

My sheep had literally been the recipients of my life. It had been shared with them abundantly and unstintingly. Nothing was ever held back. All that I possessed was in truth poured out unremittingly in order that together we should prosper. The strength of my young body, the keen enthusiasm of my spirit, the energy of my mind, the alertness of my emotions, the thrust and drive of my disposition were all directed to the well-being of my flock. And it showed in abundant measure.

This is the graphic picture our Lord had in His mind when He stated simply, "I am come that they might have life, and that they might have it more abundantly. I am the good shepherd: the good shepherd giveth his life for the sheep."

If we pause to reflect here a moment we must see that any person is "good" in whatever he undertakes to the degree in which he devotes and dedicates himself to it. A "good violinist" becomes a good violinist only by putting his time, talents, and attention into his art and instrument. Likewise a "good runner" becomes a top athlete only to the extent that he will invest his strength and energy and interest in his sport. And the degree to which anyone becomes "good" is the length to which he will go in giving unhesitatingly to his chosen vocation.

Thus, in speaking of our Good Shepherd we are compelled to consider the enormous generosity with which He gives Himself to us without stint. The very nature and character of God, exemplified in Christ, convinces us beyond any doubt that He literally pours Himself out on our behalf. All of the eternal, ongoing activities and energetic enterprises of God have been designed that we might share His abundant life.

We are not, as the people of His pasture, merely the recipients of good gifts which He dispenses to us in random fashion from afar. To think this way is to be terribly impoverished in our lives.

For much of my early Christian life I labored under this delusion. To me God was a distant deity. If perchance I needed extra strength or wisdom or patience to face some perplexing problem He who resided off in the immensity of space somewhere could be appealed to for help and support in my dilemma. If my conduct was commendable He would probably, hopefully cooperate. He would condescend to comply with my requests. If all went well He might just drop down a bit of wisdom or strength or patience to meet my need for the moment.

To imagine or assume that this is abundant life, or abundant living, is a caricature of the true Christian life. Yet multitudes of God's people struggle along this way. Their lives are impotent and impoverished because of it.

The simple truth is that the abundant, dynamic life of God can be ours continuously. It is not something handed out in neat little packages as we pray for it sporadically.

A man or woman has the life of God to the extent that he or she has God. We have the peace of God to the extent that we experience the presence of Christ. We enjoy the joy of the Lord to the degree we are indwelt by the very Spirit of God. We express the love of God to the measure we allow ourselves to be indwelt by God Himself.

God is not "way out there somewhere." He is here!

He not only resides within anyone who will receive Him, but equally important is the fact that He completely enfolds and surrounds us with His presence. He is the essence of both our inner life and outer life. "O God, You are here! O Christ, You have come that I might have abundant life. O gracious Spirit, You are as invisible as the wind yet as real as the air that surrounds me, which I inhale to energize my body! You are within and without.

"It is in You, O my God, that I live and move and have my being. You are the environment from which my total life is derived. You are the energy and dynamic of my whole being. Every good and every perfect bestowal is derived from You. The vitality of my spirit, the energy of my emotions, the drive of my disposition, the powerful potential of my mind, the vigor of my body; in fact, every facet of my total, abundant life is a reflection of Your life, O Lord, being lived out in me and through me."

To become aware of this is to become charged mightily with the abundant life of God, in Christ, by His Spirit. This is to experience being "in Christ," and "Christ in me." This is to *know* God. This is to enjoy eternal life, the life of the eternal One being expressed through my person. This is, as Paul put it, "knowing Christ and the power of his resurrection."

This life of God, given so freely to us in an undiminished supply from an inexhaustible source, is not intended to end in us. We are not an end in ourselves. The abundant outpouring of God's life to His people is intended to be an overflowing, out-giving, ongoing disposal of His benefits to others around us. More than this, it is designed to bring pleasure, delight, and blessing back to our Lord Himself. It is not just a case of His blessings being bestowed on us, but also our abundant lives in return being a blessing to Him.

> Bless the LORD, O my soul: and all that is within me, bless his holy name. Bless the LORD O my soul, and forget not all his benefits.'' (Ps. 103: 1-2)

The full and complete awareness of this concept of abundant Christian living can come to us only as we grasp the nature and character of God, our Father. The Scripture reveal Him to be love. By that is meant not a selfish, self-indulgent, sentimental love, but its opposite.

The love of God spoken of so extensively is total selflessness. It is God, in Christ, sharing Himself with us unhesitatingly. It is He giving Himself in glad, wholehearted abandonment to us. It is God pouring Himself out for His people. It is God losing Himself in our little lives that we might know the abundance of His life. It is God giving Himself to us without measure in overflowing abundance so that in turn His life spills out from ours to go running over our weary old world in streams of refreshing.

The life of God comes to us in many ways. So majestic and marvelous are they that this little book cannot begin to list or catalog them all. The life of God given to men is the same life that energizes the entire cosmos. It sustains the universe. It is the essence of being.

The best a mere mortal can do is to go quietly to some place, still, alone, there to meditate before the splendor of our God.

I sense something of His glory in the wonders of the world He made: the flaming sunrises and sunsets that still the soul; the awesome grandeur of mighty mountain ranges and sweeping plains; the restless roar of ocean waves and winds and tides; the fragrance of forests or the green glory of rich grasslands; the austere stillness and rugged solitude of gaunt deserts; the delicate beauty of flowers, trees, and shrubs; the incredible diversity of insects, birds, and mammals; the beauty of sun and cloud, snow and rain.

All of these contribute something to the total environment which supports and sustains me. Each in its own way contributes to the well-being of my person. They energize and feed my body. They stimulate and quicken my soul. They enrich my spirit. They make me what I am . . . a man sensitive, receptive, and alive to the world around me—my Father's world—His provision for my well-being, joy, and abundant life. He has come. He has made it all possible. He has put it at my disposal for full and enriched living.

All that is sublime, beautiful, dignified, noble, and grand has this as its source. The finest in our literature, music, arts, science, and social intercourse has its base in the generous giving of our Lord. All that contributes to our physical health, energy, and acumen as individuals is grounded in the good gifts and undiminished life of God poured out to us upon the planet.

And yet in His magnanimous and magnificent generosity He does not just leave it at that. God has deliberately chosen to articulate Himself in terms I can comprehend. He has spoken. His Word has been received, recorded, and reproduced in human writing. He has not withheld His will or wishes from us earthlings in mystical obscurity. It is possible to know precisely what He is like. He has articulated Himself in meticulous terms understandable to man. He has given us clear and concise self-revelations as to His gracious character, impeccable conduct, and friendly conversation. We know who it is with whom we have to do. He does not deal with us according to our foibles and failings, but in amazing mercy and gracious kindness, as our Father.

As though all of this is not enough, He has gone even further in coming to us as God in man. He, the living God in Christ, has come among us, wholly identified with us in our human condition and human dilemma. He has not spared Himself. He was born among us, lived among us, worked among us, served among us, taught among us, died among us, rose among us, and ascended among us to reclaim and repossess His place of prominence.

All of this He did willingly and gladly to deliver us from the plight of our own peril upon the planet. He came to set us free from the folly and foibles of our own perverseness and pride. He gave His life to redeem us from our slavery to sin and selfish self-interests and Satan. He gave Himself to seek and to save us who were lost. He came to call us to Himself. He came to gather us into His family to enfold us in His flock. He gave Himself to make us His own, the recipients of His own abundant, abounding life.

To those few, and they are relatively few, who have responded to His overtures, He still comes, even today, and gives Himself to us by His gracious Spirit. He is with us. He is our counselor. He is our companion. He is our "alongside one." He is our comforter. He is our closest friend. He is here in rich and wondrous intimacy.

"I am come that you might have life, My life, and that you might have it in overflowing abundance." These are still His words to us today.

❧ 10 ❧
"The Hireling"

But he that is an hireling, and not the shepherd, whose own the sheep are not, seeth the wolf coming, and leaveth the sheep, and fleeth: and the wolf catcheth them, and scattereth the sheep.

The hireling fleeth, because he is an hireling, and careth not for the sheep. (John 10:12-13)

OUR LORD USED contrast for dynamic effect. It was one of the secrets of His remarkable, arresting teaching. He used contrast to display in bold, bright strokes the great truths we human beings have such difficulty in comprehending.

He told about the rich man and the poor beggar Lazarus who lay at his doorstep. He recounted the incident of the haughty, proud Pharisee praying while the contrite publican struck his breast begging for mercy. He contrasted the prodigal with his very "proper" elder brother. And now, in this parable, Christ brings before us the behavior of a hireling as it is contrasted with the Good Shepherd in caring for sheep.

Our Lord previously pointed out how the people of God's pasture could, under His control, enjoy an abundant, rich life with Him.

He made clear how God's life, poured out in rich measure on my behalf, enables me to enjoy abundant living in every area: physical, mental, moral, emotional, and spiritual. He told how life in Him contributes to a wholesomeness and holiness of unique quality; that it is entirely possible for a man or woman to be so intimately associated with God as to reflect His character to a skeptical society.

Yet, in bold contrast to all of the foregoing, Jesus made it clear that not all sheep were under a good shepherd. Some suffered because of the bad behavior of hireling shepherds.

During the time of our Lord's sojourn in Palestine, servants were of two sorts. They were either bond or free. They were either slaves owned outright by their masters or free people who worked temporarily for meager wages. In fact, because of slavery, the worth and dignity of a human being was much less esteemed than it was in a free society. After all, if people could be bought and sold at random in a slave market they were really not of much more value than cattle or furniture.

It will be recalled that when Judas bartered with the high priests for the betrayal of his Master, the price of thirty pieces of silver was agreed upon. This was the going price, then, of a slave in the slave market.

If a slave served his owner well and the two became attached to each other, the master often offered to set him free. The slave could then choose either to go free or become a bond slave or bond servant. Of his own free will he could choose to remain, for the rest of his life, as a servant who, because of his love for the master, chose to remain in his family.

To confirm this the owner would take his slave to the doorpost of his home. Placing the slave's ear against it, he would pierce the lobe with an awl, pinning it momentarily to the post. This drew blood. This indicated that a bond was sealed for life, and that this slave had in fact become a love servant for the remainder of his days. He would never leave that family. He would be ever faithful to his owner. He was a part of that household. Their life was his. His life was theirs.

There was none of this devotion about a hireling. A hireling had no permanence. He was a casual laborer who came and went at will in a rather haphazard way. He would be here today and gone tomorrow. He was essentially a transient worker. He took no special interest in his job. As soon as a few shekels jingled in the deep folds of his loin cloth he was gone. He would seldom settle down or take any responsibility seriously. His average wage in Jesus' day was a penny a day. The less work he could do to earn this the better it suited him. Like a dandelion seed drifting on the wind he floated about the country looking for the softest spot to land. And if the place did not please him he would soon take off for another.

Sometimes, but not often, one of these drifters would be employed to tend sheep in the owner's absence. It was seldom a satisfactory arrangement. For that reason our Lord used the hireling to represent those who were entrusted with the sheep, but had no real love or concern for them. The secret to successful livestock husbandry is an essential love for the animals under one's care. And this the hireling lacked. He had no stake in the flock. They were not his. He could care less what became of them. They were but the means whereby he could make his "fast buck," and then get out.

As a young man of twenty-five I was entrusted with the management and development of a large livestock ranching operation in central British Columbia. There were thirty-six men on the various crews hired to run the ranch. We were in a rather remote, though choice, area, where the glamor and glitter of cities seemed far away.

Among us there was a common joke that we really had three crews: one was coming; the second was working temporarily; and the third was leaving. These were all hired men, passing through, who stayed in this remote and lonely location only until they had gathered up enough to move on to a more desirable job.

In bold contrast I recall vividly the love, loyalty, and undivided devotion of the Masai in East Africa to their animals. For the years we lived among them I never ceased to marvel at the incredible fortitude of these people in providing the best care they could for their livestock. No price was too high to pay to protect their stock from predators. Why? Because they owned them. They had a stake in them. They loved them. They were not hirelings.

Just a few days after we moved into the Masai country, a small, slim boy about ten years old was carried up to our house. He had, single-handed, tackled a young lioness that tried to kill one of his flock. In total self-abandonment and utter bravery he had managed to spear the lion. The mauling he took almost cost him his life. We rushed him to the nearest hospital twenty-seven miles away where his young life was spared, as by a thread. But why did he do this? Because the sheep were his. His love and honor and loyalty were at stake. He would not spare himself. He was not a hireling.

God has, all through history, entrusted the care of His sheep to so-called undershepherds. And not all of them have proven to be as loyal as the Masai lad, nor as brave as young David, later Israel's great king, who slew the lion and the bear that came to raid his father's flock.

Inevitably in the nature of human affairs there appear those who pretend to be genuine but are not. The ancient prophets of Israel cried out again and again against those who posed as shepherds to God's people, but who instead only plundered them for their own selfish ends.

> And the word of the LORD came unto me, saying, son of man, prophesy against the shepherds of Israel, prophesy, and say unto them, Thus saith the lord GOD unto the shepherds; Woe be to the shepherds of Israel that do feed themselves! Should not the Shepherds feed the flocks?
>
> Ye eat the fat, and ye clothe you with the wool, ye kill them that are fed: but ye feed not the flock. The diseased have ye not strengthened, neither have ye healed that which was sick, neither have ye bound up that which was broken, neither have ye brought again that

which was driven away, neither have ye sought that which was lost;

But with force and with cruelty have ye ruled them.

And they were scattered, because there is no shepherd: and they became meat to all the beasts of the field, when they were scattered.

My sheep wandered through all the mountains, and upon every high hill: Yea, my flock was scattered upon all the face of the earth, and none did search or seek after them. (Ezek. 34:1-6)

The same situation prevailed in Jesus' time. Those who posed as the protectors and leaders of the people, the priests, Pharisees, scribes and Sadduccees, were but rank opportunists who plundered and abused the people. The rake-off in the temple trade alone in Jerusalem exceeded $35,000,000 a year. Most of it went to line the pockets and oil the palms of the oppressors. Little wonder Christ went storming through the temple to clear it of its counterfeit activities shouting, "You will not make my Father's house, a place of plunder . . . a den of thieves!"

His confrontation was always with the ecclesiastical hierarchy of His times. They were not true shepherds. They did not love their charges. They did not care deeply for those in their care. They never wept over the plight of their people who were sheep gone astray. They were hirelings. They were there to grab what they could get for themselves.

Is it any wonder our Lord thundered out His great imprecations against them? Here, He the great Good Shepherd, saw His people abused and betrayed by those who had no interest in them whatever.

And the same applies to all church history since His day. God's people have always been parasitized by imposters. Men have worked with the flock only for what they could get out of it; not for what they could contribute to the well-being of their people.

It was this sort of thing that nearly ruined me as a young man. There was within my spirit a strange, powerful, deep desire to *know* God. I literally thirsted and hungered for spiritual sustenance. I longed to be fed truth that would satisfy my innermost craving.

Sunday after Sunday my wife and I would attend whatever churches we could. Some of them were small and struggling. Others were large and pretentious. Some of the preachers were proper and orthodox but seldom shepherds. Again and again I came hoping to be fed, but there was nothing.

Frustrated and angry I would storm home, and vow never to enter a church again. "I'm like a sheep going to the feed trough hoping to find hay or grain, and there is only dust and chaff!" I would storm to my gentle wife. In her wisdom, kindness, and patience she would prevail on me to keep going, for sooner or later she was sure a few straws would be found here and there.

Why was this? Because many of the men who were supposed to be shepherding God's people were only hirelings. They were in the job for what they could get out of it. It was obvious they spent no time communing with Christ. It was clear the Scriptures were not a *living* Word to them. They had no great love either for God or for His people. What happened to their charges really did not seem to matter.

Eventually some of these men came to know me personally, but even after they had entered into our lives, their casual indifference and lack of genuine concern astonished me.

In one community I attended services diligently for

117

nearly four years. At the end of that time I had been taught virtually nothing. I was a stranger in a far country, away from my home land, but no shepherd seemed to care for my soul.

At that period in my life I was under tremendous attack from the enemy of my soul. Almost daily I was exposed to onslaughts against the great truths of God's revelation in His Word. Subtle suggestions and crafty cynicism were working havoc in my convictions. The wolves were at work on me but there was no shepherd around who really seemed to be concerned about this wandering sheep.

Alone and unattended I fled for safety. I knew not really where to run. Like a sheep blinded with fear and seized with panic I simply turned to run in my own stupid way. And the result was that I went far astray. I ended up far from my Good Shepherd. The hirelings had literally let me fend for myself.

The net result can be expressed in the words of the grand old prophet Ezekiel:

> For thus saith the Lord GOD; Behold, I, even I, will both search my sheep, and seek them out.
>
> As a shepherd seeketh out his flock in the day that he is among his sheep that are scattered; so will I seek out my sheep, and will deliver them out of all places where they have been scattered in the cloudy and dark day.
> (Ezek. 34:11-12)

Only the tender compassion of Christ, only the understanding of the true Shepherd of my soul, only the gentle overtures of the gracious Spirit of God could ever retrieve this wild and wayward one from the cloudy and dark days of his despair. Because in His patience and perseverance He pursued me along my wayward path, because He gathered me up again and drew me back once more in selfless love, was I saved. And for this I shall be eternally grateful to my God.

But what desperate despair I could have been spared if only someone had cared for my soul at that stage of my life. Those to whom I looked for help were only hirelings. They would not stand up to the enemy. They would not engage the wolves that were raiding my life and the lives of others. They would not risk a confrontation. They simply turned tail and left us to be torn and scattered.

The same is still true. There are ministers, teachers, scholars, writers, and leaders who pose as champions of Christianity. But when the enemy comes in they are shown in their true colors. They back away rather than risk a confrontation. They settle for withdrawal rather than beard the lion or bear, or assail the wolf.

They turn and flee in the face of violent attack. Others remain silent while their people are deceived, harried, and driven to despair. Only the Good Shepherd cares enough for His own to lay down His life for them.

It must be He who, living His life through and in His true undershepherds, enables them also to lay down their lives for the sheep. They must be prepared and willing to be expendable for the sake of others. They are not hirelings, they are His slaves of love. Paul calls himself "a bondservant of Jesus Christ."

Men or women who enter God's service should regard this as an enormous responsibility not only before God but also to those whom they serve. It is something which is not undertaken lightly or casually for personal gain, but with an eye to eternal consequences.

In any enterprise where we are co-workers with

Christ there is incumbent upon us the obligation to realize that this is not a hit-or-miss affair. His view of His work in the world is a sincere and serious one. And He expects that those who enter His enterprises will take a similar attitude.

When we give ourselves to serve the Lord, the primary motivation should not be one of personal gain or advantage. Rather, the predominant desire ought to be one of serving the Master out of love and gratitude for His goodness to us. We are freely, willingly choosing to be a benefit to others, not just for their sakes or our own self-gratification, but for His sake.

It is only the undershepherd, whose first and foremost devotion and consecration is to Christ, who can stand up to the strains and stresses of shepherding. If one's devotion is only to people, deep, disappointing disillusionments are bound to come. But for the one whose service is centered in Christ there comes the strength and serenity to meet all the storms.

We love Him because He first loved us.

We love others because He first loved us.

We love at all because He first loved us.

This is what it means to be a love slave and not a hireling.

⁂{ 11 }⁂

The Shepherd
Knows His Sheep
and
They Know Him

I am the good shepherd, and know my
sheep, and am known of mine. (John
10:14)

IN ALL OF Scripture this must surely be
one of the most reassuring statements
made by our Lord to His people. Oh,
the wonder and joy of being known by
God! The strength and consolation of
being in the care of Christ who fully
and completely understands us!

Such awareness and such knowing stills
our spirits, soothes our souls, and fills us with quiet
awe. "O God, You do know me through and through."

The ultimate measure of a good shepherd is how
well he knows his sheep. Just as we might say that the
measure of a good artist or a good gardener or a good

121

mechanic is the extent to which he "knows" the materials with which he works.

This "knowing" implies much more than just mere acquaintance or contact with sheep. It means the shepherd is so familiar with his sheep, has handled them so much, that he knows their every trait, habit, and characteristic. He can predict their behavior under any given set of circumstances. He understands all their peculiarities. He is never surprised or taken aback by their unusual idiosyncrasies. He is at ease with them, comfortable in their company, delighting in their management.

The full impact of this unique relationship between livestock and their owners came home to me with enormous impact during the years my family and I lived among the Masai people of East Africa. These nomadic livestock owners believed implicitly that to them, and only them, had God given the original responsibility for husbanding livestock.

The Masai were tremendously proud of their supposed management skills with sheep and cattle. They entertained a haughty superiority toward anyone else who tended stock. And much of their claim to fame in this field was based on their knowing individual animals intimately.

In part their pride was justified. The animals under their care were their very life. They gave themselves to them with unstinted devotion. No demand was too tough nor any risk too hazardous to insure their well-being. They would go to any lengths, day or night, to protect them and care for them.

But over and beyond all this lay the incredible intimacy and personal awareness each owner had for his own charges. Many of the lambs, kids, and calves had been hand reared within the affection of the family circle. They were fondled, hugged, caressed, and called by cute pet names. Bonds of enduring affection were forged from birth that the ensuing years could never break.

Again and again I would watch, awe-struck, as one of the Masai would go up to one of his favorite beasts in the field and spend time caressing it. He would speak to it in endearing terms. He would examine and scrutinize it carefully, checking to see that all was well. This was not something done only on rare occasions. It was a normal part of the appealing relationship between shepherd and sheep.

Some of the fondest memories that came back to me from those years on Africa's sun-drenched plains are wrapped up in small boys shepherding sheep. I can still see them holding lambs gently in their arms. I can see them calling to their pets who came running at the sound of their voices. I can see the obvious pleasure and delight with which the sheep reveled in this attention. They sensed and knew all was well when they were in their owner's embrace. Here was safety and assurance. They were known.

When we turn our attention to our own lives in the care of the Good Shepherd we discover some powerful parallels. If we can grasp them they may well revolutionize our whole relationship to God.

It is essential for us to face the fact that God has known us from our earliest beginnings. By that I do not mean just collectively as a race of people upon the planet, but in a much more private and personal way as an individual human being from the hour of my conception in my mother's womb.

Such knowledge alone startles some of us.

123

In fact some find it alarming.

Amid a society where, especially in large urban centers, it is possible to live almost anonymously, this is shattering.

We in the western world have become extremely skilled at living behind a false facade. We wear masks. Seldom do we disclose our true identity. We try to present a brave front to the world, even though within we may be shattered, broken people. We proceed on the assumption that most people really don't know us and don't care. We often run a bluff on others, based on the premise that they will not or cannot be bothered to really find us out.

The net result is that for many, life becomes a sham. It is almost play acting. It is played by people playing little games with each other. Much of it is really make-believe. It lacks depth, honesty, or sincerity. People become phonies, they are riddled with skepticism and cynicism. They really don't know where they are at.

Against this background of confused and bewildered life God steps onto the stage and states dramatically, surely, and without apology, "I know you! I understand you! I have known all about you all the time!"

Just the thought of such "knowing," of such insights terrifies most people. In their phony pretense they want to run, to flee, to escape, to hide behind their masks.

But for others of us, this knowing comes at long last as a great relief, a great release from our restless roaming. "O Lord," our spirit cries out, "at last I have been found. Now I am found out. I am known! I can step out of the shadows of my own stumbling steps into the full splendor of Your knowledge. Take me. Search me. Examine me carefully. Put me right. Let me be Yours. And please, You be mine!"

It is only when a person sees himself as known before God that he will get serious with Him. Until this happens we go on playing our pathetic little games with Him. We behave as though we were indeed doing Him a great favor to allow Him to draw near. What colossal conceit! What incredible stupidity. How long will we delude ourselves?

In contrast David, himself a shepherd, cried out exultingly in Psalm 139

> O LORD, thou has searched me and known me. Thou knowest my downsitting and mine uprising, thou understandest my thought afar off. Thou compassest my path and my lying down, and art acquainted with all my ways. For there is not a word in my tongue, but, Lo, O LORD, thou knowest it altogether. Thou hast beset me behind and before, and laid thine hand upon me. Such knowledge is too wonderful for me; it is high, I cannot attain unto it. Whither shall I go from thy spirit? Or whither shall I flee from thy presence? If I ascend up into heaven, thou art there: If I make my bed in hell, behold, thou art there. If I take the wings of the morning, and dwell in the uttermost parts of the sea; Even there shall thy hand lead me, and thy right hand shall hold me. If I say, Surely the darkness shall cover me; even the night shall be light about me. Yea, the darkness hideth not from thee; but the night shineth as the day: The darkness and the light are both alike to thee. For thou hast possessed my reins: Thou hast covered me in my mother's womb. I will praise thee; for I am fearfully and wonderfully made: marvellous are thy works; and that my soul knoweth right well.
>
> (vv. 1-14)

Before such affirmations we are stilled. In wonder and joy we are awed. "O Great, Good Shepherd of my soul, how wondrous to know that You know me!"

For the Christian this awareness can become a potent power in his walk with God. An enormous desire to be open and honest with his Master will descend upon him. The mask will be removed from him by the Spirit of God as He works in his life. A sense of earnestness and simple sincerity will replace the superficiality of his former life style.

He will take God seriously. He will begin to obey His Word. He will be sensitive to the voice of His gracious Spirit. He will allow no petty pride or other obstacle of self-will to obstruct the movement of God's Spirit in his life. He will allow himself to come under Christ's control.

In contrast to the world's way of working, God, by His Spirit, begins to do His work at the center of our beings. The world's view is that if an ideal environment of better housing, hygiene, health, and nutrition is supplied, along with improved education, man will become better and better. History has repeatedly demonstrated the fallacy of this idea.

God's approach is the opposite. His gracious Spirit touches and enlivens man's spirit. If allowed to, He will illuminate the whole inner life. He will permeate the total personality transforming the dispostion, emotions, and mind. The net result will be that the remade man will alter his whole environment.

A good environment does not guarantee good men.

But noble men do generate an improved environment.

So God's Spirit begins His re-creative work within us by touching our spirits. He makes us alive to what is right and what is wrong. He impresses upon us what we "ought to do" and what we "ought not do."

We become acutely God-conscious. We are aware of what He wants. We know His wishes. We are alerted to His aims and ambitions for us.

This is what it means to have a Christian conscience. We wish to cooperate with Christ. He knows us. We know Him. We have common interests.

Likewise in the area of our communion with Him, we begin to discover that there can be an ongoing discourse between us. He speaks to me. I speak to Him. This intercourse finds full expression in prayer, praise, petitions, and personal awareness that He is ever present.

It takes time to do this. It is profound. It cannot be hurried or rushed. The man who would know God must be prepared to give time to Him.

It is tremendously helpful to speak privately but audibly to the Lord. Let Him know you love Him, that you are fond of Him, that you are deeply grateful for all His kindness.

Not long ago I visited an elderly lady who claimed she had known Christ for more than thirty years. I asked her if she enjoyed conversing with Him quietly in the privacy of her own elegant home. I inquired if she ever told Him how much she loved Him.

Her response was an outburst of embarrassed laughter. "Oh," she blurted out blushingly, "only you would ever suggest such a thing, Phillip." But I left her home wondering just how well she really knew the Good Shepherd.

In his first epistle the apostle Peter put it this way: "Unto you therefore which believe he is precious" (1 Peter 2:7).

Why? Because I am His and He knows me through and through. And even though He knows the worst,

He still loves me with an everlasting love.

This knowing is the great central theme that runs like a chord of gold all through John's first epistle. To know the love of God. To know that we have His life. To know that He hears us. To know that we belong to Him, etc.

Such knowledge is strength. It is stability. It is serenity. It is the solid assurance upon which my relationship to the Good Shepherd stands secure.

There is nothing ambiguous or vague about it. There are no ifs, maybes, perhaps, supposes, or assuming it may be so. I know!

As the Spirit of Christ expands His influence within my life He will begin to penetrate my personality. If allowed to do so He can pervade my mind, emotions, and disposition.

No doubt the ultimate, acid test of Christianity is the dramatic and beneficial changes wrought in the personality and character of people. Weak become strong. Deceivers become honest. Vile become noble. Vicious become gentle. Selfish become selfless.

Perhaps the area in which there is the most cover-up is that of our minds. Most people live very private thought lives. Even within the intimate family circle it is possible to retire and withdraw into the inner sanctum of our minds and imaginations.

Were some of the scenes there enacted, to be exposed, it would shock and startle our family and friends to find what sort of world we moved in mentally.

It is sobering to realize, "O God, you know all my thoughts." It is equally solemnizing to remind ourselves always, "And, O God, I know You know!"

This is a purifying discipline. In the presence of His

impeccable person it humbles, cleanses, and converts me, turning me from the wickedness of my ways to walk softly in His sight.

As He is allowed to move into my emotions the same process is at work. The same eternal promise holds true. There can be no pretext, no pretense, no playing around, pretending to be so pleasant or pious while within we seethe and boil with pent-up perverseness. "O Lord, You know me!"

With other human beings ill will, hatred, bitterness, envy, old grudges, jealousy, and numerous other heinous attitudes may be masked with a casual shrug of the shoulder or forced half smile. But we simply cannot pull the wool over God's all-seeing eyes. We may kid ourselves that we are getting away with the cover-up, but we don't kid God.

Over and over, when our Lord moved among us as a man, He emphasized the importance in His estimation of our inner attitudes. They were the ultimate criteria to a man's character. He simply could not tolerate false pretenders, who, though appearing to shine like mausoleums in the sun, were filled with dead men's bones.

"O God, You know my anger, resentment, impatience, hostility, and many other evil emotions; I know You know."

What is the solution? Somehow my soul must be cleansed. The debris and dung of a thousand terrible thoughts and imaginations must be swept from my life. It is my sins and iniquities which have come between me and my God. Where is the solution?

I am ever reminded of Hercules who was given the impossible assignment of cleansing the gigantic Aegaen stables. Thousands of horses had deposited their dung within its walls until a literal mountain of manure engulfed the place.

Hercules knew full well, even in his own great strength, that he could never remove the accumulated filth. Instead, he went high into the hills and there found a rushing mountain stream. He diverted it from its course and directed its clear flowing waters through the huge stables. In a short time the surging stream had flushed away all the dung. The stables stood clean because of the sparkling water from the high country.

It is a sublime picture of the wondrous work God's gracious Spirit can effect in a Christian's life. Only as He is allowed to surge freely through the rooms and galleries of my inner life can they ever be cleansed from the dark thoughts, the evil imaginations, the angry emotions, and evil decisions of my disposition.

If in open honesty and genuine earnestness I come to Christ and open my person to Him, He will come in. He will penetrate every part of me. He will purify. He will fill with His presence. His peace will permeate me. His power will be mine in inner strength.

This power will enable me to make proper decisions. His presence at work within me will empower me to both will and do His good pleasure. I shall find harmony and unity between Him and myself. There will be common purposes, common aims, common joys we share. Why? Because He knows me and I know Him.

These titanic changes which can be effected within my spirit and soul by God, can likewise be accomplished in my body. It is He who designed and fashioned men and women in all of their complexities. He knows and fully understands all the instincts, desires, and appetites of our physical make-up.

As we allow ourselves to come gently and increasingly under His control, we will find it affects how we handle our bodies. They will be nurtured and treated with respect. They will not be abused or misused. We will find it possible to so discipline ourselves and direct our activities that even in our bodies there will be a blessing, and that not only a benefit to us but also a benediction to others.

It is possible for God's people to live in moderation, wisdom, and exuberant joy. We can so conduct ourselves amid a corrupt society and sick culture that we are a credit to our Master.

We can practice moderation in our daily habits. It is as much God's good will for me to eat wholesome food, drink pure drinks, enjoy regular rest, revel in regular exercise, and relish the beauty of His creation as it is to go to church. All is sacred and sublime when touched by the delight of His presence with me.

I do not know Him only within the confines of a cathedral. I do not meet Him only within the pages of a Bible or in the still moments of meditation. I can encounter and commune with Christ my Shepherd anywhere along the long winding trails of life that we walk together.

My walk with God need not in any sense be a spectacular display of special dedication. It need not have any carnival atmosphere about it to be convincing. I don't have to indulge in theatrics to impress either Him or other human beings.

What He desires most is that I walk with Him humbly, quietly, and obediently. The communion between shepherd and sheep is sweet and secure because *He knows me* and *I know Him!*

One Flock
of
One Shepherd

As the Father knoweth me, even so know I the Father: and I lay down my life for the sheep. And other sheep I have, which are not of this fold: them also I must bring, and they shall hear my voice; and there shall be one fold (flock), and one shepherd. (John 10:15-16)

THIS IS AN appropriate point at which to pause for a moment in studying this parable. Always it is important to keep in mind a clear picture of the setting in which our Lord made His statements.

A young man was born blind. His eyesight was restored by Christ and then he discovered who his benefactor was. In his incredible gratitude the healed man rejoiced not only in new-found physical sight, but also in new-found spiritual sight. He actually *saw*

Jesus as his great deliverer, his Savior, his Redeemer.

Though he had been excommunicated and cut off from any further association with the religious leaders, this was only a small loss—for he had found the Christ. He had come to know Him who could give great meaning and direction to his previously derelict life. In humble awe he believed. And with touching appreciation he worshiped Jesus, bowing down before Him in glad submission.

This act of obeisance scandalized and horrified the Jews. They were infuriated even further when the Master made it clear that it was in fact they, who thought they saw and knew and understood spiritual realities, who were blind. The accusation enraged them. Like a pack of bloodhounds closing in on their prey, they encircled Him, bent on His destruction. Their blood boiled. Their eyes blazed with hate.

This next statement Jesus makes—"As the Father knoweth me, even so know I the Father"—was outrageous enough that they charged Him with being utterly insane, if not possessed of a demon.

Of course, it was proof positive of their own self-delusion. They stood confronted by the One who was the light of the world but whose presence only accentuated their own dreadful darkness. They were encountering heaven's royalty in disguise. Yet they rejected God's anointed Prince of Peace with impassioned pride. He who stood encircled by them came from God, knew God, was very God, but they were totally blind to His being.

In just a few more moments they would pick up rocks from the ground ready to break His bones and dash out His brains. If they could not still Him with spiritual arguments, they could slay Him with stones.

Men forever try to silence God, but He does not go away that easily. He always has the last word.

It was not within man's power, nor will it ever be, to do away with God. If His life was to be put on the line, it would be at the time of His own choosing and in the manner of His own choice. No man would deprive Him of this honor or privilege. Jesus later made this clear to His would-be assassins.

What so enraged them was His claim to divinity. "I know the Father. The Father knows me." There was nothing vague or tenuous about this intimate relationship. It was not a knowing of hearsay or second-hand acquaintance. It was in truth a knowing of the most profound, personal sort. It implied the interaction of coequals, the unequivocal unity of total oneness. Jesus, in His final statement to His foes on this important occasion, said, "I and my Father are one!"

This straightforward claim to deity completely undid His audience. And it has been the stone over which uncounted millions have stumbled since.

Unless we grasp the profound and enormous implications of this claim of Christ to being known and knowing God, all the other remarks made later will have no relevance. I say this in sincerity to remind the reader that our Lord was not just a good man; He was also the great God in human guise. His claims to a special knowledge and relationship with His Father were recognized by the Jews as outright insistence on His personal deity.

Not only were they unwilling to accept Him as such, but the same has been true for most men during the past twenty centuries.

If we are to "see," if we are to "understand," we must face the formidable fact that this One was none other than God. He was the God of the Godhead who knew from before the creation of planet earth what plans were made to preserve and restore human beings to a proper relationship with Himself.

He was the God who would have to identify Himself with men in their darkness and dilemma of despair and deception. He would have to interpose His own pure and impeccable life on their behalf, as a substitute for their grievous sins that incurred the judgment of a righteous God. He who knew no sin, of necessity had to be made sin with our wrong doings, in order that we might be made right with His amazing righteousness.

Only as He Himself, in His own person, exhausted and absorbed the penalty for our wrongs in His death, could we be acquitted and set free. This freedom to be His, to follow Him, to become the people He intended, must of necessity be bought for us at an appalling price.

The price paid was His own life. It was His righteous, sublime life poured out as a supreme propitiation for our pride, perverseness, and pollution. This satisfied the awful abhorrence of a selfless God for our selfish sins, but also delivered us from death, alienation, and the despair of our dreadful dilemma.

Like the young man born blind, only a tiny handful of human beings have ever seen or grasped this truth.

In his simplicity and sincerity he had allowed the great Shepherd of his soul to enter the fold of his young life. He had allowed Him to take control. He had allowed the Good Shepherd to claim him as His own.

The cost to him, too, had been great to come into the care of Christ. His contemporaries had cut him off

136

from the synagogue. They had ostracized him from their company. They had heaped scorn and abuse upon him. He had done no wrong. His only misconduct was to come into Christ's care, to become one of His flock.

The flock of God has never been very large. Our Lord made it clear few would come into His care.

Most of us are sheep who turn to our own way and go astray.

Yet scattered across the world are those who are His.

Down the long avenues of human history the Good Shepherd has been out among us, gathering up those who would come.

With enormous compassion and great tenderness He looked at the young man whose sight had just been restored. "Other sheep I have, which are not of this fold." All over the earth there are other lives, individual sheepfolds, scattered like so many sheep astray, whose intimate folds He is eager to enter. This young man's life was but one tiny fold out of uncounted thousands which in their sum total would make up His final flock.

It is important to recognize the difference between a flock and a fold. The shepherd is said to have only one flock. This flock is the sum total of all the sheep which belong to him. But almost always his flock is distributed widely, especially if he is a wealthy owner, among many folds across the country. Put another way, we can say that one sheepman's flock is made up of many different folds. The modern rendering of John 10:16 is much more accurate than the King James version which confuses the reader by stating "There shall be one *fold*," rather than, "There shall be one *flock*," which is correct and clear.

When we lived among the Masai people of East Africa it impressed me how one livestock owner would have his animals scattered in small groups all across the countryside. One very wealthy man whom I came to know quite well actually owned more than 10,000 head of stock. But these were not all cared for in one place. They were distributed in little clusters here and there, scattered widely among many kraals.

Yet, the sum total of them all comprised his one unit, one herd, one flock under one owner.

It will help the reader to understand this concept if we look at modern farming practices on the prairies. During pioneer days it was common for each individual family to own and operate its own homestead. These small holdings of land comprised either a quarter (160 acres) or half (320 acres) section of land, a full section being one square mile or 640 acres.

With the advent of power equipment and expensive machinery most farmers found they needed more land to justify the investment made in expensive tractors, plows, drills, and combines. The upshot was that the more prosperous and efficient farmers began to buy up random quarter or half sections their neighbors might sell them.

The final result has been that today one man's farm may well include numerous pieces of land scattered all across the country at random. Yet he refers to them in total as "my farm."

I knew of one wealthy grain grower who owned seventeen different quarter sections. Separately, each was a unit of its own. Collectively they comprised his one farm. The same is true with sheepmen. All their folds together become their one flock under one owner.

Looking now at Christ's flock, we see clearly that it is composed of many different lives (little folds) scattered at random all across the earth. He is ever active and at work bringing men and women into His care and under His control. He gathers them up from the far-flung corners of the world. He has been energetically engaged in this enterprise since the beginning of human history.

A magnificent and splendid overview of Christ's achievements through the centuries is painted for us by John in the Book of Revelation. Under the unction and inspiration of God's own gracious Spirit he writes glowingly this great song.

> You are worthy to take the scroll and to open its seals, because you were slain, and with your blood you purchased men for God from every tribe and language and people and nation.
>
> You have made them to be a kingdom and priests to serve our God, and they will reign on the earth.
>
> (5:9-10, NIV)

And so the eyes of our spiritual understanding are opened to see our Good Shepherd, relentlessly, tirelessly, eagerly calling to Himself those chosen ones who will respond to His voice and come to His call. He brings them in from every tribe, every language, every race, every nation.

His majestic voice has rung out over all the earth. In unmistakable sounds He calls out to any who will come. With enormous compassion He cries out to men "Come unto me, all ye that labour and are heavy laden, and I will give you rest."

None other has ever extended to wayward wanderers such a winsome, warm invitation. But most men spurn it. They turn instead each to their own per-

139

verse path that leads into peril and ultimately to perdition.

Yet from out of earth's milling masses a small flock is being faithfully formed. We find members of that flock scattered here and there. By no means are they confined to any one church, denomination, or sect. Rather, they are distributed widely, and spread rather thinly through a multitude of groups and gatherings of diverse doctrines.

It has been my great privilege through the years of my long life to have rich fellowship with other Christians all over the world. My travels have taken me to some forty different countries. The places where I met other people who knew Christ as their Good Shepherd would take a whole book to describe fully. I have stood solemnized in some of the most impressive cathedrals ever erected by man and there sensed and known that others of His flock were with me in the care of Christ. By the same measure I have sat in tiny mud huts in Africa and grass thatch houses in southeast Asia where the Good Shepherd had also gathered up some of His sheep.

You see, the ultimate criteria is not the church, the creed, the form of communion, or even the cherished and contested claims to special spiritual insight which determine a person's position. It is simply this: "Do they or do they not hear Christ's voice?"

He Himself said emphatically, "Other sheep I have. Them also I must bring. They shall hear My voice."

To hear Christ's voice, as was pointed out in a previous chapter, means three essential things.

1) I recognize it is God who calls me to Himself. He graciously invites me to come under His care, to be-

nefit from His management of my life, to accept His provision for me.

2) I respond to His overtures by taking Him seriously. I alert myself to act. I open my life to Him so He may in truth and reality enter to share it with me.

3) I then run to do whatever He wishes. I cooperate with His desires. I regularly do His will. Thus I enter fully into the greatness of His life, grateful for His care.

This is to "hear" Christ's call and to respond.

Any man or woman who does this belongs to Him, is a member of His flock, a sheep of His pasture. Our Lord has them here and there in ten thousand times ten thousand tiny folds, each flourishing under His infinite love.

⨳{ 13 }⨳
Christ
Lays Down
and
Takes Up
His Own
Life

Therefore doth
my father love me, be-
cause I lay down my
life, that I might take it
again. No man taketh it
from me, but I lay it down
of myself. I have power to
lay it down, and I have power to take
it again. This commandment have I received
of my Father. (John 10:17-18)

OVER AND OVER in this book the point has been made
that the hallmark of the Good Shepherd is His willingness to lay down His life for His sheep. It cannot be
otherwise. The essential nature of Christ demands it.
Because He is love, selfless love, this must be so.

This love of God is the most potent force extant in
the universe. It is the primal energy that powers the
entire cosmos. It is the basic driving initiative that lies
behind every good and noble action. Without it all
men of all time would languish in despair. They would
grope in darkness. Ultimately they would know only

separation from the goodness of God which is death.

But—and it is a remarkable "but"—Christ was willing to leave His glory; to come among us expressing that love, giving tangible form to it in a sacrificial life. I have written of this love at great length in *Rabboni*. Here I quote from its pages without apology: "With our finite minds we cannot probe but a short distance into the vastness of Christ's pre-earth existence. But with the enlightenment that comes to our spirits by His Spirit we sense and feel the magnitude of His enterprises in arranging and governing the universe.

"Such enlightenment comes from His Spirit. He the Eternal Spirit of the Infinite God; the same Spirit of the Eternal Christ; was simultaneously in everlasting existence with both the Father and The Son, Our Christ. He like them was engaged in the enormous activities that long preceeded even the appearance of the planet earth.

"In all the enterprises which engaged this tremendous triumvirate, there was perfect coordination of concept and ultimate unity of purpose in their planning. Unlike human endeavours there was never any discord. Friction was unknown simply because there was no self-interest present. Between God The Father, God The Son (Jesus Christ) and God The Spirit, there flowed love in its most sublime form. In fact this love was of such purity that it constituted the very basis of their beings. It was the essence of their characters.

"We earth men can barely conceive of a relationship so sublime that it contains no trace of self-assertion, no ulterior motives for self-gratification. But that is the secret to the strength of God. Here was demonstrated the irresistible force of utter self-lessness. In the total giving of each to the other in profound 'caring' for each

144

other lay the love of all eternity. This was love at its loftiest level. This was love at its highest source. This was love, the primal source of all energy.

"Just as there is stored within an atom enormous power because of the inter-action between neutrons, protons and electrons, likewise there was inherent unlimited energy in the Godhead because of the inter-relationship between Father, Son and Spirit. And the essence of this energy was love.

"In that outer world love was the moving force behind every action. Love was the energizing influence at work in every enterprise. It was the very fabric woven into every aspect of Christ's life. It was in fact the basic raw material used ultimately to fashion and form all subsequent matter.

"To the reader this may seem a bit obscure, a bit beyond belief. But if we pause to find parallels upon our planet, earth, we may soon see the picture in practical terms. What is the most irresistible force upon the earth? Love? What pulverizes strong prejudice and builds enduring allegiance? Love? What binds men together in indestructible devotion? Love? What underlies all generous and magnanimous actions? Love? What is the source of strength for men and women who gladly serve and die for one another? Love? What energizes the loftiest and most noble enterprise of human hearts and minds? Love? If this be true of selfish mortal men, then how much more is it the very life of God—And this is the life of Christ.

"It was in the setting of a realm permeated by love that the generous thought of sharing it with others came into being. Of course it could scarcely be otherwise. For if heaven was such a happy home it would scarcely have been consistent for God to want to keep

145

it to Himself. Love insists on sharing.

"So the concept was born of love that other sons and daughters should be brought into being who could participate in the delights of paradise. That such a remarkably generous endeavour was even considered is in keeping with the character of God. He chose to do this in love and out of love simply because of who He is.

> Praise be to God and Father of our Lord Jesus Christ for giving us through Christ every possible spiritual benefit as citizens of Heaven! For consider what he has done—before the foundation of the world he chose us to become in Christ, his holy and blameless children living within His constant care. He planned, in his purpose of love, that we should be adopted as his own children through Jesus Christ—that we might learn to praise that glorious generosity of his which he has made us welcome in the everlasting love he bears toward his Beloved.   (Eph. 1:3-6, *Phillips*)

"Like all other divine enterprises it undoubtably first found expression in the mind of God The Father. Yet it was agreed to completely by God The Son and fully endorsed by God The Holy Spirit."

All of this Christ did deliberately, freely, gladly out of His own generous good will toward us. It was not that we deserved or merited such magnificent mercy, but it was because of His own inherent character. He really could not do otherwise. There was nothing in us to earn His gracious attention. *The only compulsion upon Him was the compulsion of His own wondrous love.*

Are we surprised then that it is for this reason He stated He was loved so dearly by God the Father. This love was not and never can be anything soft or sentimental or insipid. Rather, it is strong as steel,

146

tough as tungsten, yet glittering with the incandescent brilliance of a diamond.

It had to be for Him to endure the abuse and calumny of His earth days at the hands of wicked, selfish men. His entire interlude upon the planet represented the utmost in ignominy. Born into a peasant home, surrounded by the appalling filth of an eastern sheepfold, His birth could not have been more debasing. The long years of His youth and early manhood were spent in the most wicked town in Palestine. Nazareth was notorious for its wicked ways. Yet there He toiled, sweated, and hewed out a meager living working in wood to support his widowed mother and siblings.

He lived in abject poverty without a home to call His own. He literally laid Himself out for others. His strength and stamina flowed out to those who followed Him. His great vitality restored the sick, raised the dead, fed the masses, ministered to those in sorrow, and propelled Him from one end of the country to the other with incredible energy. Everywhere He went, men and women sensed the touch of His strength, the impact of God's love upon them.

Inherent in Christ in perfect poise were the divine life of undiminished deity and the delightful life of untarnished humanity. Though He was the suffering servant, He was also the magnificent Lord of glory— God, very God.

At His death this became supremely evident. In that terrible agony of the garden, in the ignoble lynching by the mob under cover of darkness, in the atrocious trials and beastly behavior of men determined to destroy Him, in the crucible of His cruel crucifixion, He emerges ever as the One in control. He chose to die this way. He chose deliberately to lay down His life in this manner. It was all His doing and His dying for dreadful men.

No matter what the scoffers and skeptics may say, He stands at the central crossroads of human history as its supreme character. No other individual, with so little ostentation, so shaped the eternal destiny of men.

But His death was not His end. It was but the conclusion of a magnificent chapter in the story of God's plan for man.

Death could not hold Him. Decay and decomposition could not deteriorate Him. The spices and wrappings and grave clothes that enfolded Him were for naught. They were powerless to prevent His resurrection. With majesty and growing grandeur He took His place of power. His position of omnipotence was reinstated. His coronation as King of Kings and Lord of Lords was celebrated in the throne room of eternity.

All of this Jesus foreknew and declared fearlessly to the young man born blind. He stated these facts with calm assurance to any who would listen—the Pharisees, Scribes, and others who now encircled Him.

They knew full well what it was that He implied. He was in truth telling them that He was none other than God. He was declaring unashamedly that He, their Messiah, the anointed One of God, their Promised One, was now among them. He had chosen to come to His people. It would be but a brief sojourn, and then He would return to the splendors from whence He came.

But why had He come? Why suffer? Why lay down His life? Why endure such agony for sinners?

Because men were lost. And His commission from His Father was that He should come to seek and to save those who were lost. He knew this to be His unique responsibility in the redemptive enterprises of God. He recognized it was His responsibility to carry out and execute in precise detail this executive order of the Godhead.

His audience then, and most men ever since, refused to believe they were lost. In truth it is exceedingly difficult to convince human beings that they are in peril. Like the Scribes and Pharisees of Jesus' day, we are prone to pride ourselves upon our religiosity, our cultural achievements, our educational attainments, our material possessions, or any other attributes which we naively suppose are indicators of our success in living.

We who are in the family of God, who have been found by the Good Shepherd, often seem to forget just how "lost" we really were. As we look out upon a confused society and bewildered world we allow its trappings and trumpetings to blind us to the lostness of our families, friends, or acquaintances. We are dazzled by the glittering exteriors and flashing facades put on by people in desperate peril away from God. Fine language, impressive homes, beautiful cars, elaborate furnishings, glamorous holidays, affluent incomes, sharp clothes, and clever minds are no criteria for having either succeeded or found the reason for our being. We can have all these and still be far from God.

This explains why God, in Christ, by His Spirit, continues to pursue men. His approach to them polarizes people. He is willing to lay down His life for them in order that He might also take it up again in them. Some are delighted to discover He has drawn near, ready to pick them up in His own strong arms. Others turn away, go their own way, and refuse adamantly to have anything to do with Him. To those who respond He gives Himself in wondrous ways.

> Behold, the Lord GOD will come with strong hand, and his arm shall rule for him: Behold, his reward is with him, and his work before him.
>
> He shall feed his flock like a shepherd: he shall gather the lambs with his arm, and carry them in his bosom, and shall gently lead those that are with young.
>
> (Isa. 40:10-11)

What a remarkable portrait this is of our Lord, laying down His life for His sheep. He feeds them; He leads them gently; He gathers them up in His strong arms; He carries them close to His heart.

It is in this way that He also takes up His life again in us. Caught up into His care, encircled by His strong arms, enfolded within His love, we find ourselves *in Him.* This is part of the great secret to sharing in His life.

Much more than this, however, is the fact that it is to Him an endless source of satisfaction. He looks upon the outpouring of His life, the travail of His soul, the generous giving of Himself repaid and returned in sons and daughters brought to glory. Men and women, retrieved from their utter lostness and dereliction, are restored to the grandeur of wholesome godliness and new life in Him.

Often as I let my mind wander back to the great storms and blizzards that we went through on my ranches I recall scenes full of pathos and power. Again and again I would come home to our humble cottage with two or three tiny forlorn, cold lambs bundled up against my chest. They would be wrapped up within the generous folds of my big, rough wool jacket. Outside hail, sleet, snow, and chilling rain would be lashing my face and body. But within my arms the lambs were safe and sure of survival.

Part of the great compensation for enduring the blizzards, fighting the elements, and braving the storms was to pick up lost lambs. And as I picked them up I realized in truth I was taking up my own life again in them; my life that had been expended freely, gladly on their behalf.

It is as I am found in Him that He, too, revels and rejoices in my being found. No wonder there is such rejoicing in heaven over one lost soul who is brought home.

Sad to say, many of Jesus' hearers did not and could not understand. In fact, they went so far as to say He was insane.

PARABLE III

John 10:25-30

CHRIST IN ME AND ME IN CHRIST

14

To Believe in Christ Is to Belong to Christ

Jesus answered them, I told you, and ye believed not: the works that I do in my Father's name, they bear witness of me.

But ye believe not, because ye are not of my sheep, as I said unto you.

My sheep hear my voice, and I know them, and they follow me. (John 10:25-27)

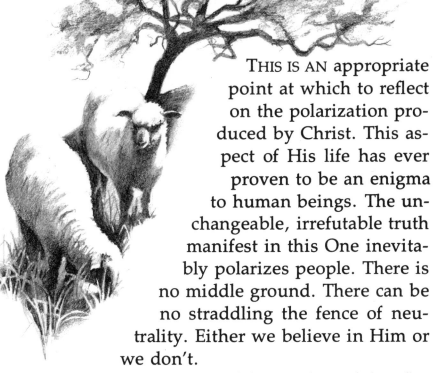

THIS IS AN appropriate point at which to reflect on the polarization produced by Christ. This aspect of His life has ever proven to be an enigma to human beings. The unchangeable, irrefutable truth manifest in this One inevitably polarizes people. There is no middle ground. There can be no straddling the fence of neutrality. Either we believe in Him or we don't.

Perhaps polarization should be explained briefly. Whenever truth, that is to say absolutes, or eternal verities are presented to a person they produce one of two reactions. The first reaction is that the soul and spirit in search of God responds positively and promptly. There is an immediate move toward the truth. The spirit lays hold of, and takes to itself, the verities presented. They become a veritable part of one's life. They are the vitalizing, energizing, invigorating life of God moving into human character, human conduct, human conversation. They change, color, and condition a person until he is conformed to Christ.

The alternative is the opposite; it is a negative reaction. The end result is a rejection of truth, which of course implies ultimately the rejection of Christ.

This was eminently true in His days upon earth, and it is the same today. And on this occasion his attackers went so far as to declare Him either a raving maniac or one possessed of a devil. Eventually their animosity and reaction to Him became so violent they schemed to destroy Him. Several times He slipped through their clutching fingers, but eventually, like bloodhounds, they brought Him to bay. Nor were they satisfied that He was stilled until they saw Him suspended on a cruel Roman gibbet. There, hanging midway between earth and sky, writhing in agony, they were sure His disquieting and disturbing declarations would terminate in His death.

But truth simply does not die that way.

Truth does not disappear in the face of evil.

Truth is indestructible just as God is indestructible.

Truth endures forever.

Truth remains eternal.

So down the long avenues of time men have turned angrily amid the darkness and despair of their dreadful deeds to attack truth. They have derided it, despised it, and tried to demolish it. Or better, we should say that in their blindness and ignorance they have so desired. Why?

The clearest and most concise answer to that enormous, unending question is given by Christ Himself:

> For God so loved the world, that he gave his only begotten Son, that whosoever believeth in him should not perish, but have everlasting life. For God sent not his Son into the world to condemn the world; but that the world through him might be saved. He that believeth on him is not condemned: but he that believeth not is condemned already, because he hath not believed in the name of the only begotten Son of God. And this is the condemnation, that light is come into the world, and men loved darkness rather than light, because their deeds were evil. For every one that doeth evil hateth the light, neither cometh to the light, lest his deeds should be reproved. But he that doeth truth cometh to the light, that his deeds may be made manifest, that they are wrought in God. (John 3:16-21)

On this particular occasion our Lord's adversaries ranted and raged at Him. "How long are You going to keep us in doubt?" "If you really are the Christ tell us plainly!"

The pathetic aspect of the whole scene really was their own positive refusal to accept what He had said as truth.

Repeatedly He had declared His identity. They knew from their familiarity with the Old Testament Scriptures that this One who now stood before them was none other than the promised Messiah. He was God's Anointed. He was the Great, Good Shepherd foretold by the prophets and seers of their people. David, Isaiah, Ezekiel and others had predicted that the true

Shepherd would come to gather up and restore the lost sheep of Israel.

Over and over Christ had asserted that He was in fact that One. He was here. The Good Shepherd was among them. He was calling to His own. He was gathering them up . . . those who would come.

But they adamantly refused to believe Him.

They simply would not accept Him.

They rejected and repudiated all He said.

Yet, over and beyond all of this He endeavored to convince them of His credentials by repeated demonstrations of His deity.

He performed all sorts of remarkable miracles that were positive proof and incontestable confirmation of His divinity. They had heard Him preach good tidings to the meek and poor. They had watched Him bind up the broken-hearted. They had seen Him liberate those who were captive to evil spirits, disease, or their own deranged minds and emotions. They had been there when He spoke comfort to those who mourned. They had seen sorrow turned to gladness.

They had been witnesses to the full and total fulfillment of all that Isaiah predicted in 61:1-3

> The spirit of the Lord GOD is upon me; because the LORD hath anointed me to preach good tidings unto the meek; he hath sent me to bind up the broken-hearted, to proclaim liberty to the captives, and the opening of the prison to them that are bound; To proclaim the acceptable year of the LORD, and the day of vengeance of our God; to comfort all that mourn; To appoint unto them that mourn in Zion, to give unto them beauty for ashes, the oil of joy for mourning, the garment of praise for the spirit of heaviness; that they might be called trees of righteousness, the planting of the LORD, that he might be glorified.

And still they would not believe. Still they would not receive Him.

Accordingly it is absolutely essential for us, as it was for them, to grasp fully what it really means "to believe," "to receive," for by Christ's own simple statement He insisted that only those who do believe belong to Him.

"To believe" implies much more than merely giving my mental assent to truth. It is much more than merely agreeing to what God has to say.

There are literally hundreds of thousands of people who profess to be believers who do this much. They agree in a formal manner to the truth as it is revealed in the Scriptures. They subscribe in a rather ambiguous way to the teachings of Christ. They believe that in some rather obscure way He was a historical character who came to earth to reveal truth to us. He was really no more than another of the great prophets or teachers who claimed divine attributes and abilities.

But this simply is not enough!

Even the evil spirits believe this much and tremble.

Without a doubt the greatest single weakness in Christendom the world around is so called "believism." It is an anachronism that millions who claim to believe are in reality a repudiation of the living Christ. Their characters, conduct, and conversation are a living travesty of the truth they claim to exemplify.

This is why Christianity and the church is eternally being charged with hypocrisy. It is why so many who are outside claim that those inside the church are charletans. It is why to be a true believer is difficult, simply because so often the behavior of our so-called brethren betrays them and us. We are all lumped together and labeled as imposters. And our dilemma only deepens when all around us, amid the confusion and criticism, men and women insist they are all believers, when in truth their behavior may well be a reproach to Christ.

In our Lord's discourses He equated believing with drinking. To believe truth, to believe Him, was in fact to imbibe truth, to imbibe him.

> . . . He that believeth on me shall never thirst.
> (John 6:35)

> If any man thirst, let him come unto me, and drink. He that believeth on me, as the scripture hath said, out of his belly (innermost being) shall flow rivers of living water. (John 7:37-38)

To believe in Christ is not just to give endorsement in an objective manner to what He has done and said on my behalf.

To believe in Christ is to fully accept both Him and His truth so that I actually take Him into my life in deliberate, volitional action, that goes on continuously.

Put another way it means this: He, the living Christ, is actually allowed to so enter the whole of my life that He shares it with me, lives it with me, becomes an integral, vitalizing part of it. In other words, He is in me and I am in Him.

The closest parallel to this is marriage.

It is possible to read about marriage, talk about it, discuss it, and debate it. But until you find another whom you implicitly trust and love enough to invite into your life to share it with you, you know virtually nothing about the truth of all that marriage implies. It must be experienced to be known. It must be tried to be understood. It must be undertaken to be enjoyed. It must be engaged in to be believed.

It is the same with Christ. He is referred to in Scripture as the Bridegroom and we His bride.

The second closest parallel to this is the intimate interrelationship between a shepherd and his sheep.

We can discuss shepherding, read about it, study it, observe it, and even enjoy watching it. Yet until we actually participate, we really know nothing about it except in a very remote, detached, and impersonal way.

And this is precisely the point Jesus made when He said: "You don't believe, simply because you don't actually belong to Me. You aren't My sheep."

All through this book and also in *A Shepherd Looks at Psalm 23*, I have endeavored to point out in unmistakable language what it really means to "belong" to Christ. I have tried to show what is involved in "coming under Christ's control." I have indicated the great joys and benefits and advantages of allowing our lives to actually be managed by Him who made us, who bought us, and who is legitimately entitled to own us.

Yet, the point must be made again here that the decision as to whether or not this will happen rests with us. Christ comes to us. He calls to us. He invites us to turn to Him. He offers to take us under His care. He longs to lead us in His ways. He desires to share life with us. He wants us to enter fully into the joys of His ownership. He delights to give us all the advantages and benefits of His life.

In short, He wants to be in our lives and for us to be in His.

Are we or are we not prepared to have this happen?

It is an intimate association from which most of us

161

shy away. We really are afraid of this involvement. To speak of "believing" in this way makes most of us uneasy. We are not at all sure we wish to be so completely committed. There is so much at stake! Yes! all of this life; all of eternity; all of myself is at stake.

It is only the person prepared to become open and available to God, who positively responds to truth as it is revealed in Christ, the Great, Good Shepherd, who will "hear" His voice.

To hear Him is to "recognize" that this One is in truth none other than God, very God.

This being so, what He says and what He does will be taken seriously. We will respond to Him in powerful ways of acceptance and total personal commitment.

Evidence of this will be apparent in a deliberate and eager willingness to do whatever He requires. This "running" to do His bidding demonstrates faith and confidence in Christ of a potent sort. This is to believe in Christ—to know God!

It is this intimate interchange and private interrelationship between Christ and me that becomes such a unique relationship. It is in truth the "knowing," of which Christ as the Good Shepherd speaks with such affection. He is in my life; I am in His. He knows me; I know Him. He is mine; I am His.

This is a precious relationship. The acute awareness that He knows me and I know God in Christ is the most profound and potent influence I am privileged to know as a man. In its awareness lies great rest.

There is about this knowing an element of elevation that induces me to attain lofty living and noble conduct far beyond anything I might otherwise have thought possible. This knowing is the powerful, potent presence of the very person of Christ made real in my everyday experience by His gracious Spirit.

Finally, there is the inescapable reality that this knowing has a profound purifying effect upon my life in all its activities. I live and move and have my being in company with Him who is altogether noble. He is royalty. He is my Lord, my Owner, my Master, and in His close company I scorn that which is corrupt.

Only those who know Him in this manner, who believe on Him to this extent, who receive Him without reservation in this way find it appropriate to follow Him.

I have used the word appropriate deliberately here. It implies that to follow Christ, as following Him has been explained previously in this book, is not something absurd or unrealistic or unreasonable. Rather, to follow Him becomes the proper, reasonable, and appropriate thing to do.

To follow Christ means I become intimately identified with His plans and purposes for the planet and for me as a person. His wishes become my wishes. His work becomes my work. His words become my words. His standards, values, and priorities become mine. His interests become my interests. His life becomes my life.

In a word: He is in me; I am in Him. There is the place of peace. Here lies serenity, strength, and stability amid earth's troublous times.

❖❧ 15 ❧❖
Eternal Life in the Hands of the Shepherd

My sheep hear my voice, and I know them, and they follow me:

And I give unto them eternal life; and they shall never perish, neither shall any man pluck them out of my hand. (John 10:27-28)

AT THE HEAD of this chapter, John 10:27, 28 have been deliberately set down together. They cannot be separated. These verses constitute one continuous concept.

The incredibly beautiful relationship between the Shepherd and His sheep can be and only is possible provided the sheep hear His voice, are known of Him in intimate oneness, and so follow Him in quiet, implicit confidence.

165

The eternal life inherent in Him, whereby they shall never perish, within which they can enjoy endless security under His hand, are benefits made possible only in constant communion with Him.

If we turn our attention to a human shepherd and his sheep we will see this to be self-evident.

Those sheep which remain in the shepherd's personal care are the ones which derive and draw their very life from his provision and possession of them. They have at their disposal all the resources of his ranch. They thrive under the expertise of his skilled management. They enjoy the eternal vigilance and loving protection of his care. Under his hand they flourish because they are "handled" with affection by one who is tremendously fond of them. In fact, they are his very life. In turn he becomes to them their very life.

Looking back in gentle reminiscence across the distant years of my own life as a sheepman this remains its most memorable aspect. There was a profound and deeply moving sense in which all my life, all my strength, all my energy, all my vitality was poured into my flock. It simply had to be so if they were to enjoy an optimum life under my management.

The "life" which they had in such rich measure and overflowing abundance was but an expression of my own life continuously given to them day after day. The lush green pastures, the lovely wooded parkland where they could shelter from summer sun and winter winds, the clear cool water to slake their thirst, the freedom from predators or rustlers, the protection against disease and parasites of all sorts, the loving attention and intimate care of one who delighted in their on-going well-being all reflected my own life lived out through them.

They came to be known and recognized uniquely as being "Keller's sheep." They had upon them the indelible, unmistakable mark of belonging to me. Their health, quality, and excellence were a declaration of whose they were.

Yet, it must be emphasized that this life, this special care, this exquisite sense of security and well-being was theirs only as long as they remained on my ranch and under my hand.

In my book on Psalm 23 I told in detail of certain sheep which were never really satisfied to stay in my care. They were always looking for a chance to slip out through a hole in the fence. Or they would creep around the end of the enclosure that ran down to the seashore at extreme low tide. Once they had gotten out, they were exposed to enormous perils. Some wandered far off to become lost up the road or into the woods. And there they fell prey to all sorts of disasters.

With all of this in mind our Lord made it clear that our own relationship to Him is the same. The remarkable eternal life which He gives to us is His own life transmitted to us continuously as we remain in close contact with Him. His vitality, His vigor, His view of things are mine as long as the communion between us is constant.

It is a mistake to imagine that eternal life, the very life of the risen Christ, is some gift package dropped into the pocket of my life at some specific point in time; that once it has been bestowed I automatically have it forever.

Life, any kind of life, physical, moral, or spiritual, simply is not of that sort.

Life is correspondence between an organism and its

environment. Life goes on only so long as the organism is deriving its sustenance from its surroundings. The instant it no longer draws its support from its environment, life ceases. At that point the organism is declared to be dead.

This principle applies in the realm of my body—physical. It holds true in the region of my soul—moral. It is so in my spirit—spiritual.

All of life originates with God irrespective of whether it be physical, moral, or spiritual. To assume that He bestows only spiritual life to human beings is a distortion of truth.

The whole of the biota, the total physical, chemical, and biological environment which supports my physical body comes from Him. He designed it. He programmed it. He set it in motion. He sustains it. He maintains its meticulous functions. He enables me thus to derive my physical life and well-being from His wondrous world around me. The moment I can no longer do this I am said to be physically dead.

Precisely the same principle operates in my soul. My mind, emotions, and will are stimulated and sustained by correspondence with the moral environment that surrounds me. This is the realm of human relationships and ideologies. It is the world of ideas, concepts, and culture expressed in literature, science, the arts, music, and accumulated experience of the human race.

A person can be acutely, vividly alive to all of this. Or he can be likewise virtually dead to it. For some it is well nigh life itself. Yet even here every capacity anyone has to correspond or communicate with this total soulish environment comes from God. It is He who has arranged, ordered, and programmed all that is excellent, beautiful, and noble in the arts, sciences, and humanities. Man has only just gradually uncovered all that formerly lay hidden from his restricted vision.

So in truth, all moral, all soul life is derived from our Lord, for without the capacities of mind, emotion, and will bestowed upon us by Him, we would have no way of enjoying even this life.

Again, it may be legitimately stated that the moment I can no longer derive moral stimulation and uplift from this realm I am said to be dead to it. What is more, it is perfectly possible to be physically alive yet morally dead to one or more or all of God's life in this region.

I am said to be morally alive only so long as I draw life from those generous and godly gifts bestowed upon me by a benevolent and loving Master. He so designed me as to live on this noble lofty plane as His person.

What has been said of physical and moral life also applies in the region of my spirit. There, deep within my inner life, lies my conscience, my intuition, and my capacity to commune with God by His Spirit.

I am said to have spiritual life only so long as there is being derived directly from God a measure of His life. It is He who in the realm of my conscience alerts me to absolute verities, ultimate truth. It is in this way I know what I ought to do, what I ought not to do. I am alive to what is appropriate and proper behavior before Him and what is not.

It is in the realm of my intuition that I enjoy that ultimate dimension of living, in knowing God. It is in the unique awareness of being alive to Him that I enjoy life at its loftiest level. There steals over my stilled spirit the sure knowledge that it is in Christ I live and move and have my being. This is to know also that I am known of Him, intimately, personally, and with profound affection.

So there flows between His gracious Spirit and my spirit an interchange of life—His life. I am in Him; He is in me. There is an ongoing, continuing interrelationship whereby He imparts His life to me and takes up my little life into His.

To know, experience, and enjoy this communion with Christ is to have eternal life. This is what Christ meant when He said unashamedly, "I give unto them eternal life."

He went on to add emphatically and with great emphasis, "They shall never perish."

As long as my communion with Him continues, His life is imparted as a clear flowing stream from the fountain source of His own magnificent, inexhaustible self. He comes to me continuously in never-ending life to energize and invigorate me. I am His, to be the recipient of an ever-renewed life. He is mine to be the bestower of every good and perfect gift needed to sustain me through all eternity.

He has no other intention than that this relationship should be one of eternal endurance.

My part is to remain ever open, responsive, and receptive to the inflow of His life to mine. It is His life that surrounds and enfolds me on every side. In any situation, at any time, in any place I can breath quietly, "O Christ, You are here. You are the ever-present one—the great 'I Am.' Live Your life in me, through me, in this moment, for I, too, am in Your presence ready to receive You in all Your splendor."

The person who so lives in Christ's presence shall never perish. He it is out of whose innermost being cascades clear streams of life-giving refreshment to those around him. This is the individual who is an inspiration and blessing to his generation, and to his God.

Those who live this joyous and serene communion with Christ are the men and women who know they are in God's hand. Nor will they ever make a move or entertain a thought that would take them out of His hand.

To know that God's hand is upon me for good is perhaps the most precious awareness a human being can savor in his earthly sojourn. To be acutely aware—"O my Shepherd, You are enfolding me in Your great strong hand!"—is to sense a sweet serenity that nothing can disturb. To realize the intimacy of the Master's touch upon all the minutiae of my affairs, to experience His hand guiding, leading, directing in every detail of each day, is to enter a delight words cannot describe.

My part is to be sensitive to His gentle Spirit. My part is to obey instantly His smallest wish. My part is to wait quietly for the unfolding of His best purposes and plans. In harmony, unity, and mutual pleasure we commune together along the trails of life. He becomes my fondest friend and most intimate companion. More than that, He becomes my life.

This is the life of serene security. This is the relationship of quiet relaxation. This is the life of rest and repose; for the person willing to be led of the Lord there is endless enjoyment in His company.

The ancient prophet Isaiah portrays this for us in an exquisite word picture of the Great Shepherd of our souls.

> O Zion, that bringest good tidings, get thee up into the high mountain; O Jerusalem, that bringest good tidings, lift up thy voice with strength; Lift it up, be not afraid; Say unto the cities of Judah, Behold your God! Behold, the Lord GOD will come with strong hand, and his arm shall rule for him: behold, his reward is with him, and his work before him.
>
> He shall feed his flock like a shepherd: he shall gather the lambs with his arm, and carry them in his bosom, and shall gently lead those that are with young.
>
> (Isa. 40:9-11)

It has always been our Lord's intention to hold His people in His own strong hand. It is the most profound longing of His Spirit to lead us gently in the paths of right living. He is eager and happy to gather us up into His powerful arms where no harm can molest us.

The intentions of God toward His own are always good. He ever has their own best interests at heart. His desires are only for their well-being. He is a Shepherd of enormous good will and deep compassion for the people of His pasture.

It is ever He who holds us in His hand, if we will allow ourselves to be so owned and loved. We do not have to "hold on to Him" as so many wrongly imagine. How much better to rest in the quiet assurance of knowing His hand is upon me rather than doubting my feeble efforts to hold onto Him.

This is one of the great secrets to a serene life in Christ. It does not come instantly, overnight so to speak. It is the gradual outgrowth of a life lived quietly in gentle communion with Him.

Imperceptibly there steals over my spirit the assurance that with Him, all is well. He makes no mistakes. He is ever here. And so long as I remain acutely aware of His presence, nothing can separate me from His love and care.

> Who shall separate us from the love of Christ? shall tribulation, or distress, or persecution, or famine, or nakedness, or peril, or sword? As it is written, For thy sake we are killed all the day long; we are accounted as sheep for the slaughter. Nay, in all these things we are more than conquerors through him that loved us. For I am persuaded, that neither death, nor life, nor angels, nor principalities, nor powers, nor things present, nor things to come, Nor height, nor depth, nor any other creature, shall be able to separate us from the love of God, which is in Christ Jesus our Lord.
>
> (Rom. 8:35-39)

❧❧ 16 ❧❧

The Good Shepherd Is God!

My Father, which gave them me, is greater than all;
and no man is able to pluck them out of my Father's
hand. I and my Father are one. (John 10:29-30)

THERE ARE OCCASIONS on which it is imperative that an
author share his own inner struggle in search of spiritual truth. For all of us there are sections of the Scriptures where we have found difficulty in arriving at
veracity. All of us are pilgrims on the path, and no

matter how sincerely we endeavor to follow our Good Shepherd, there are times when we stumble.

For me the two verses above, taken together, "seemed" to pose an insurmountable problem. In verse 29 our Lord states that His Father "is greater than all." In almost the next breath He asserts He and His Father are one.

The false cults who eternally deny the deity of Christ have capitalized on this "apparent" contradiction. In fact, it is a passage they exploit to the maximum in order to undermine the faith of those who have placed their simple confidence in Christ as God, very God.

It was not until I undertook a deep study on this section that at last the clear light of its meaning began to break through. What previously was puzzling has now become exceedingly precious. And it is with distinct joy and a sense of triumph that the closing chapter of this book can be written.

Once more light has replaced darkness, love has taken the place of despair. The result is that I am much richer for it, and I trust you the reader will be as well.

In Dr. Weymouth's remarkable translation this reads, "What my Father has given me is greater than all, and no one is able to wrest anything from my Father's hand. I and the Father are one."

In the translation by Knox the meaning is made even more clear. "This trust which my Father has committed to me is more precious than all else; no one can tear them away from the hand of my Father. My father and I are one."

What is this trust of such supreme importance?

What is this enormous responsibility?

What is greater than all else in God's estimation?

Wonder of wonders, and marvel of marvels, it is His

own keeping of His own sheep!

This disclosure humbles my spirit and draws me to Him with bonds of love stronger than steel, tougher than tungsten.

To realize that from God's standpoint the most precious thing is the preservation of His people, those who have come to put their confidence in Him, who have come under His control, overwhelms our hearts. In response to such compassion and caring for me there springs up within my soul an overflowing stream of gratitude. "O my God, how great You are! O my Shepherd, how wondrous are Your ways!"

I really know of no other declaration by our Lord that so stills my spirit in quiet adoration and gentle awe. To know that though I am weak and wayward and often downright difficult to handle, to Him who loves me I am very precious and this pulverizes my pride and draws me to Him.

There is something tremendously touching in this truth. It strips away all the misgivings I may have about belonging to the Shepherd of my soul. It overwhelms me with confidence and joyous assurance. "O Christ, to You I am precious! O great Shepherd, to You I am special! O Father, to You I am the supreme object of Your care and affection! I have been accepted, beloved, and wanted above all else."

Is it any wonder that He will do everything possible within His power to preserve and keep me in His hand? Am I surprised to see that the supreme price paid for my reconciliation to Him, was paid gladly and freely with His own life. It was His precious blood shed so willingly for us that now makes us so valuable. It is His touch upon my life and its transforming power to take a wayward sinner and change him into a joyous son that makes me so precious to Him.

It is not who I am that makes me special to God.

Rather, now, it is *whose* I am that makes me precious.

There is no intrinsic merit in my makeup that He should esteem me as someone significant. In fact, the opposite is the case, for by His revelation He declares me to be undone before Him.

But bless His dear name, it is the impact of His life upon mine that makes all the difference. It is the immense emancipation of His salvation that sets me free to follow Him. It is the joyous sharing of Himself with me by His Spirit that empowers me to do His will. It is the strong touch of His mighty hand upon my life that changes my character, alters my conduct, and conforms my life style to His.

This is to become His person. This is to become the sheep of His pasture. This is to become a member of His family. This is to enjoy an exquisite, intimate relationship in which I am His and He is mine. No wonder then that to Him I am exceedingly precious.

Of course, to our contemporaries we may not seem to be very special. In fact, some may even look upon us with a jaundiced eye, calling us "odd," "religious fanatics," or even "square." But let us never forget that they do not see us as God does. They can, at best, observe only our outward appearance and behavior, whereas our Shepherd knows us through and through. And though knowing even the worst about us still loves us with an enduring love—because we are His.

This truth came home to me with tremendous impact as a young man when I started to build up my first sheep ranch.

Because all my life previously I had worked with

cattle, sheep seemed strange and unfamiliar. So I sought expert advice and help from anyone who would give it to me. I was determined that I would keep only the finest stock and breed the best animals it was possible to produce. There would be no half-way measures. My sheep were special and would become increasingly precious.

I went to see an elderly, white-haired, highly esteemed sheep breeder who lived about thirty miles away. He was a Scot, who, like so many livestock men from Scotland, stand tall among the world's finest breeders of quality animals. Gently and graciously he led me out to his fields where his flock was grazing. In a small pasture about a dozen superb, big, strong rams were resting in the shade.

An endearing look of comingled love, affection, pride, and delight filled his soft brown eyes as he leaned on the fence rail letting his gaze run over his rams.

"Well," he said softly, "pick out whichever ram you wish, son." He smiled at me warmly, "You are just a young man starting out with sheep. I want you to have the best!"

I replied that only he knew which was the finest ram. It was he who had poured the long years of his life and skill and expertise into these sheep. It was he, who, with infinite care, patience, and perseverence had selected those which ultimately would become the finest stock on the whole continent. Only he knew which was the most valuable ram in his possession. Only he knew how great and precious it was to him.

Not hesitating a moment he swung open the gate with his big gnarled hands and strode in among the rams. Quickly he caught hold of a fine, handsome ram with a bold, magnificent head and strong conformation.

"This is Arrowsmith II," he said, running his hands gently over the ram. "He is the supreme Grand Champion Suffolk Ram and has won all the top awards across the country!" He rubbed the ram's ears softly in an affectionate caress. "No one else has ever handled him but me. He's my top prize ram . . . tremendously valuable . . . more than that . . . very precious to me in a very personal way!"

I could understand exactly what he meant. I was not surprised to see a misty look steal across his eyes. And I considered it one of the greatest honors of my life that he would permit me to take the ram home to become the top sire for my flock.

That day it came home to me with great clarity that what made the difference between one sheep and another was the owner. In whose hand had they been? Who was responsible for breeding, raising, and shepherding them? Was it a grand flockmaster? Was it a superb sheepman?

And so it is with us. Are we in God's hands? Who is handling us, shaping us? Whose are we? Whose life is molding mine?

Jesus said, "I and the Father are One!" It matters not whether we speak of being in the hands of God our Father, or under the control of Christ our Good Shepherd, or guided gently by the gracious Holy Spirit; we are inevitably in the hands of God.

To us today this is fairly understandable. We accept this concept without question. To us who believe He is precious (1 Peter 2:7).

But in speaking to the Pharisees, His straightforward declaration that He was one with His Father immediately alienated His audience. His simple, honest, legitimate claim to deity antagonized His hearers. He was declaring Himself to be God, very God, and they determined to destroy Him for it.

On that dark day when the mob grabbed up rocks from the ground to stone Him, they recognized that He had answered their query: "If Thou be Christ—tell us plainly!"

He had, and they rejected His claim.

He said He was One with God the Father, and they were furious.

He had come to them as the Good Shepherd, prepared to lay down His life for His sheep, but they would not have Him.

Only two young people from among this angry, hostile crowd had responded to His invitation: the young woman taken in adultery and the young man born blind. Both had felt the touch of His hand on their lives. Both had turned to Him for restoration. Both went on from there exulting in a new dimension of life. They were remade in the Shepherd's care.

The same choice still confronts mankind.

The majority still spurn the Good Shepherd.

Yet to those who hear His voice, respond to His call, come under His care, follow Him, His commitments come true. They find life, overflowing life, fulfilling life, and they find it in rich measure. It is *life in Christ and Christ in them*.